Pathways to Work

Pathways to Work

Unemployment Among Black Teenage Females

Phyllis A. Wallace
Massachusetts Institute of Technology

Lexington Books
D.C. Heath and Company
Lexington, Massachusetts
Toronto   London

Library of Congress Cataloging in Publication Data

Wallace, Phyllis Ann.
Pathways to work.

Bibliography: p.

1. Youth—Employment—New York (City) 2. Negro Youth—Employ-
ment. 3. Women, Negro. I. Title.
F130.N3W34   331.3'4'097471   73-15924
ISBN 0-669-91280-8

Published simultaneously in Canada.

Printed in the United States of America.

International Standard Book Number: 0-669-91280-8

Library of Congress Catalog Card Number: 73-15924

Table of Contents

List of Figures and Tables

List of Figures

List of Tables

Preface

Many persons have worked with me on this project, but I am especially indebted to the young black women in Central Harlem and Bedford-Stuyvesant who were members of the study group. My colleagues at the Metropolitan Applied Research Center (MARC), Drs. Kenneth B. Clark and Hylan G. Lewis, provided both tangible and intangible support. Dr. Patricia G. Morisey served as special consultant to the project; Ruth Harris Soumah was director of field activities; Donna M. Cowan, Marguerite Smith, Laura E. Tandy, Edith Brown Bryant, Linda Cole, Claudette Jenkins, and Barbara James established and maintained those links that determine success or failure on a social research project.

Dr. Howard Rosen, Director, Office of Research and Development, Manpower Administration, US Department of Labor, encouraged us to examine the sociopsychological perspectives on unemployment among black teenage females. William Paschell and Eugene Johnson of the Manpower Administration were patient project advisors. Lillian C. Christmas typed the final manuscript.

We hope that our recommendations reflect not only our concerns, but the plight of young black women who seek employment in today's labor markets.

Cambridge, Massachusetts
October 1, 1973

Pathways to Work

1

Summary

The entry of American youths into the labor force has been characterized as an unsystematized and largely haphazard process. Middle-class youngsters, however, move from nonwork to work status with considerable assistance from parents and formal and informal institutions. For young black women from poor families, however, the transition to work is exceedingly difficult.

The exploratory study by the Metropolitan Applied Research Center (MARC) of unemployment among black female teenagers in two urban poverty neighborhoods in New York City demonstrated that it is possible to provide resources to enable these young women to enter and to take continuous steps to remain in the labor market. The interactive mechanism was a peer group network. Its central activity was the strengthening of the youth themselves in developing job orientation for themselves and others. The network involved youth and family, youth and community and manpower agencies; and youth and employers.

Through a group process stimulation and guidance model, the study identified many structural weaknesses in several delivery systems in their nonresponse to black youth. These systems include education, social service agencies, manpower programs, and vocational guidance activities. The study also identified major employment problems of black female teenagers: systemic societal impediments, specifically the low priority accorded the black female teenager; dysfunctional reference groups; and motivations. More affluent teenagers have a variety of support systems and are able to weather many crises; poor blacks do not have this. There is a precarious balance at best, which is disturbed by recurrent practical or personal crises.

The project tapes, interviews, and discussions show that these young women whose families are poor residents of an urban ghetto are not a homogeneous group despite the similarity of their surface characteristics. However, the overwhelming evidence was that the unskilled black female teenager, whether in school or out, whether single or married, was generally regarded as a poor employment risk. In turn, these young women perceive themselves as the least preferred—the marginals of marginals—in the labor market.

The central finding of this report is that peer group support and reinforcement operate in strong and positive ways to counteract some of the negative influences from the community and the home. The participatory model that evolved from the small group sessions may be capable of altering some of the outcomes in the labor market for poor, black, young women. The labor-market-oriented peer group mechanism now needs to be tested, refined, and assessed as an intervention strategy for assisting young black women in their entry into the world of work.

2

Findings and Recommendations

Since black teenage females are among the least preferred workers in urban labor markets, they experience major difficulties in finding jobs. The MARC exploratory project on unemployment among black teenage females in two urban poverty neighborhoods of New York City attempted to identify sociopsychological variables that influence their labor market participation. We were concerned with how these young women perceived the characteristics and availability of work, the desirability of work, and their job expectations and opportunities. Although these aspects of the supply side of the market were emphasized, we recognized the major importance of demand factors. The occupational structures of metropolitan labor markets, quality of available education, level of social welfare expenditures, level of economic activity, prevailing wages, employer preferences, along with characteristics of the workers determine employment. We have not dealt with job placement, job creation, or job restructuring, which are demand elements.

Findings from the study and some tentative recommendations are discussed below.

Findings

1. Work may not be as salient to black teenage females from low-income families as social and community relationships. We are dealing with girls of an age group and household status where the family still acts as a basis of support. However, the participants in the project demonstrated their ability to understand and to accept the value of work even where there was little expectation of finding a job. (See discussion of job-seeking experience and employment follow-up in chapter 6.)

2. The teenage peer group (age sixteen to nineteen) played a powerful role in influencing work attitudes and changing work behavior of this teenage out-of-school/out-of-work population. It is clear that programs designed for this group are likely to have a better chance of success if they are integrated into the activities of the peer group.

3. Black teenage females who developed positive work orientation lacked both the information and knowledge of how to get a job. In our exploration of the institutions that bear on the work behavior of youths, we found that most of the study group were poorly served by schools, manpower, and social

3

service agencies. Because of these impediments, the young women in the study group consistently anticipated hostility and rejection in their job-seeking activities. (See discussion of schools, job referral agencies, and training agencies in chapter 5.)

4. Lack of child-care facilities for working mothers, especially teenage mothers, is a major problem in New York City. (See discussion in chapter 6.)

5. The work experiences, both negative and positive, of the parents strongly affect the work attitudes of their teenage children. Employment hardships experienced by many low-income blacks mean marginal existence for their families. Regardless of the expectations and aspirations they have for their children, many of these parents and guardians probably have difficulty in presenting enviable images of working adults.

6. Any effective program designed to improve job opportunities of black teenage females must include a strategy for changing employer hiring policies and practices with respect to this group. Regardless of jobs being offered or the experiences of applicants, many employers in New York City reject girls who do not have a high school diploma.

7. The peer group may provide positive support for many of the black teenage females who are marginal to the labor market. The work attitudes of other members of low-income families, especially mothers and boyfriends, were influenced by the employment activities of teenage girls in the project. Thus, there is a reciprocal relationship of parents and children reinforcing the work attitudes of each other.

8. Some of the girls believed that racial discrimination would bar them from securing good jobs. Certainly their experiences in seeking employment may have highlighted for them how pervasive and institutionalized are the patterns and practices of racial discrimination in employment. (See discussion in chapter 6.)

9. The survey and questionnaires have limited effectiveness as techniques of collecting data in low-income black communities. We found that small groups that featured direct and indirect observation and participant observation of individuals and groups were particularly effective. We also found that the girls could be used to gather as well as to generate data.

Recommendations

1. A model of stimulation and guidance based on these findings and experiences needs to be field tested. The project demonstrated that it is possible to provide black teenage females with resources to explore and bridges to enter the job market. They need support both prior to entering the job market and in taking continuing steps to stay in the labor market.

2. Such a model would:

    a. prepare (develop skills) and place unemployed black female teenagers in jobs;

    b. provide support and guidance for the peer group and family;

    c. invite community participation (school system, day care, manpower agencies);

    d. involve employers in the process; and

    e. remove the disincentives to employers of hiring young black women.

3. The project involved youth and their parents, youth and community and manpower agencies, and now we need to develop a means of bringing together in effective sessions youth and employers. Black teenage females are at the end of the labor market queue. They can be made more attractive to employers. All of the currently available evidence seems to indicate that employers will not hire and train disadvantaged black workers unless some kind of subsidy is given to them. We need to explore the feasibility of a "voucher plan" approach because it would permit the disadvantaged—in this case, black teenage females—to choose the type of job for which they wish to receive training. Perhaps employers thus would have a greater incentive to hire disadvantaged workers if they were subsidized. However, subsidies would be given directly to the disadvantaged workers to permit them to pay employers a portion of the total cost of hiring them or to seek training from appropriate agencies. More research is needed on how to acquire the skills training that is required prior to productive participation on many jobs.

4. Funds need to be explicitly earmarked for outreach, counseling, and guidance on education and employment for these young women. Our survey of manpower agencies in New York City revealed that black teenage females are the least-preferred clients (serviced only after adult males, welfare mothers, veterans, and teenage males). To a large extent the white teenagers are assisted in their job-seeking activities by family, friends, and community. Black female teenagers have no such sponsors.

5. One of the presumed bridges from school to work has been the guidance counselor. For the system to be effective it must be restructured and counselors reeducated and sensitized to be able to facilitate the movement of black youth into the work world at the same entry points as comparable whites. It was ascertained through discussions with the study group that the school guidance counselor services failed to serve as a bridge between school and the world of work. Many of the girls, acting upon information received from guidance counselors, later found it to be inadequate or incorrect. Many of the counselors and teachers in New York City schools do not seem to be interested in the

progress of black youths. A study on a fashion vocational high school in New York City revealed that the school—more specifically, the teachers—viewed their role as the gatekeeper to the labor market.[1] A trade teacher would be very cautious in referring a minority student for a known "white" position.

6. Our discussions with some of the school dropouts in the study group revealed that some girls were bored with school or felt trapped in rigidly structured educational systems. Others needed money for clothes, books, carfare, etc. We need to investigate more fully advantages and disadvantages of expanding the scope of work-study programs. The Twentieth Century Fund's Task Force on Unemployment of Minority Youth recently recommended that "employers, labor unions, and the educational authorities cooperate in bringing about a *substantial expansion of work/study, cooperative and related programs.*"[2]

7. All efforts to reduce employment discrimination and to improve the economic status of blacks should be scrutinized for intergenerational effects. The costs and benefits of providing equal employment opportunity should not be calculated only for those workers presently denied these rights. The work attitudes of black young women from low-income families are heavily influenced by the work behavior of their parents. To the extent that black adult workers experience more unemployment and employment discrimination, their children, especially the girls, have negative perceptions of work.

8. The passage of a child development bill could expand day care and family care facilities in New York City, particularly in the city's poverty areas. Our study of day care facilities and discussions with young mothers in the study group indicated an overwhelming lack of day care and family care facilities in New York City's poverty areas. Many young mothers indicated a desire to work, but due to an inability to find reliable care for their children were unable to accept employment.

9. For teenagers the high school diploma has become a critical factor in determining whether they may enter the labor market. Many young black women are hindered in their employment pursuits by the credential barriers. Employers should examine their certification requirements to determine if they are related to job duties and if the requirements discriminate against minority youth. Employers may infer that a high school graduate has good work habits. Characteristics which may or may not be valid by-products of successful completion of high school require more scrutiny. From what other more valid experiences may an employer identify desired characteristics in an employee?

10. Since the majority of the employment training organizations did not give priority to the problems of young black females, it is recommended that a special center be designated to deal only with the problems of adolescent workers or that several counselors in manpower establishments be assigned full time to work with the peer group network as the interactive mechanism for introducing young black women to the world of work.

3 Introduction

Aims of the Study

From June 1970 through April 1971, the Metropolitan Applied Research Center, Inc. (MARC) conducted an exploratory project on unemployment among black teenage females in two urban poverty neighborhoods[1] of New York City. The specific aims of this study were:

1. to identify critical variables—personal, family and community—which determine the nature of the participation of black teenage females in the labor force;
2. to evaluate the training and job systems and particularly the measures that were designed to improve the economic status of this group;
3. to recommend policy and program changes; and
4. to develop and field test more effective methods of collecting data on this target population.

According to the *Manpower Report of the President,* the 1971 unemployment rate for black teenagers was the highest reached since information of this type was first collected in 1954. Black teenagers accounted for 27 percent of black unemployment in 1971, compared with 16 percent in 1961. The worsening position of black youth was partly associated with their greater increases in the population. A significant increase, 44 percent, is expected in the black youth in the labor force during the decade of the seventies. Thus, no substantial reduction in unemployment of black teenagers will be achieved unless the several delivery systems (education, vocational guidance, manpower, and social services) improve their responses to needs of black youth. In a recent study, Holt, et al. have indicated that even if an aggregate unemployment rate of 3.8 percent were to be attained any time soon, black teenagers would experience rates of 25.5 percent.[2]

Although labor force participation rates for black women have traditionally been high, young black women in the sixteen-to-nineteen age group were significantly less represented in the civilian labor force than their white counterparts, young black males, or adult black women. According to the 1970 census there were approximately one million young black women sixteen to nineteen years of age living mainly in urban areas. Fifty-six percent of this population lived in the South, and about a quarter of these young women,

regardless of the region of their residence, were in the labor force. Thus, less
than a third of all black teenage females were in the civilian labor force as
compared with 45 percent of white female teenagers. In 1971 more than half
of the black young labor force participants were not enrolled in schools, while
the opposite was true for the white young women.[3]

Significance of the Study

Black teenage females constitute one of the most disadvantaged groups in
the labor markets of large metropolitan areas. For more than a decade, the
unemployment rate among black teenage females, sixteen to nineteen years
of age, has ranged from 28.4 percent in 1958 to 35.5 percent in 1971. These
rates have been more than double those for white females in the same age
group, four times the rate for adult black women, and consistently higher
than the rates for black male teenagers. During 1970, the employment opportunities for black female teenagers deteriorated even further as national unemployment rates rose for the more experienced and preferred workers and large
numbers of white females dominated the sharp increase of new entrants into
the labor force.

However, the labor force statistics do not provide a full picture of the
employment situation that confronts these young women. They constitute a
major waste of resources to the extent that they lack skills and work experience, are also underemployed in menial, dead-end jobs, have higher school
dropout rates, obtain inadequate education from de facto segregated school
systems, and must live in inferior housing in crime-infested neighborhoods.
Economic analysis of the employment problems of minority teenagers has
been restricted mainly to labor force participation rates, educational attainment, occupational distributions, wages and salaries, and other easily quanti-
fiable characteristics. Sociopsychological and attitudinal factors also affect
the unemployment situation of this youthful group. Greater understanding
of the experiences and problems of young black females in negotiating organ-
izational systems would facilitate the formulation and establishment of more
effective programs to improve their economic status.

Study Population

The study population included girls who were not working (some were
high school graduates and others were school dropouts) and girls with or
without work experience (some had looked for work and others had not).
The work cycle of teenagers differs from that of adults; and the work cycle
of black teenagers, who may be poor, may be quite different from other

groups. The girls, for the most part, did not perceive work as central to their lives. The transition from teenager to working adult is extraordinarily difficult for these youngsters.

Our study group was on the threshold of the world of work and ambivalent about moving into permanent attachment to this world. We wanted to know where they receive their information and views about jobs and the relationship of jobs to their futures. To what extent was this study population's view of work and unemployment shaped by their firsthand experience with high rates of unemployment among young black males or their parents?

The teenagers who participated in the study represented a fairly narrow social, economic, and educational range. They resided in Central Harlem and Bedford-Stuyvesant in neighborhoods that had been designated as poverty areas. During 1970-71, the unemployment rate among black female teenagers in the poverty areas of New York City was 32.9 percent. There was a 12.4 percentage point difference in citywide rates for black teenagers (both sexes) and the rate for white teenagers (27.7 percent versus 15.3 percent).[4] Thus, wherever black youngsters lived in New York City, they experienced significant difficulties in the labor market.

Pre-Project, During-Project, and Post-Project Employment Status of Study Population

It was difficult to chart a "before and after" basis of the employment status for the study group. Although the young women in both the Harlem and Bedford-Stuyvesant groups belonged to the same socioeconomic class, they were quite heterogeneous in experience, outlook, and attitude. Fifteen of the study group members have now had work experience. Table 3-1 and accompanying Figure 3-1 display the work experience of the study group before, during, and after the project. Nine of the study group members had worked prior to the project's inception, six found some type of work during the project, and ten were employed after the project was ended. However, these were not necessarily the same young women. Six of the girls who were working at the post-project period had worked in the pre-project period.

In attempting to determine who the "working girls" were, we hypothesized that the "in and out of the labor force" movement of the young women was characteristic of teenage workers.

Scope

We were particularly interested in life styles among black urban families, especially those in ghetto settings. Interaction of these families, both

Table 3-1
Work Experience of the Study Group

Group Member	Pre-Project	During-Project	Post-Project
1H		X	X
2H		X	X
3H	X		X
4H	X		
5H		X	
6H			
7H	X		X
8H	X		X
9H			X
10H	X		X
11H	X		X
12H		X	
1B	X		
2B			
3B	X		
4B	X	X	X
5B			
6B			
7B			
8B		X	X
Totals	9	6	10

Source: Project data, 1970–71.

internally and externally, was a major concern. We were interested in these questions:

1. What is the salience of work to teenagers in urban poverty neighborhoods? Does the ghetto offer them security and/or a sense of achievement among their peers? Does their concept of status differ from that of the larger society?

2. How does one get socialized to work? To what degree do these young women conform to the norms of their subculture? To what degree do they conform to the norms of the larger culture?

3. Has society established different goals for these teenagers based primarily on the poverty status of the families rather than teenage developmental needs?

4. What is the relationship between the network of friends and the girls? How does this affect work behavior?

5. Has the concept of "black identity" in any way contributed to their unemployment difficulties? Do they see their inability to get a job as caused by racism, or do they see their unemployment as their own fault, due to lack of formal training?

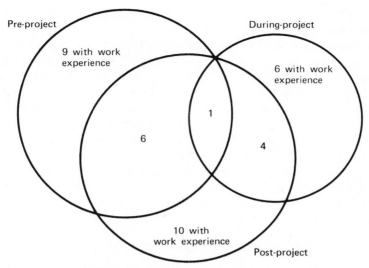

Figure 3-1. Work Experience of the Study Group

6. What values have these young women placed on the jobs they have held? Are there attractive alternative employment opportunities in the "shadow" economy of the ghetto?

7. How many of these girls are "losers" who have given up hope of bettering their conditions? Will they turn to a life involving illegal means of income, or a succession of menial jobs which they drop after a few weeks?

Sociopsychological Perspectives

On the basis of MARC's research experience and its staff's familiarity with the impact of poverty, long-standing unemployment, dysfunctional school systems, and pervasive discrimination, a number of substantive and methodological issues were considered in initiating the project.

We considered the extent to which both unemployment and employability are socially defined and socially determined. We aimed for insight into the relationship between young black female attitudes, behaviors, and actual participation in the labor force, and environmental characteristics. These included family, peer group, and community variables, as well as the objectives, characteristics, and behaviors of the systems through which these teenagers were expected to enter the labor force. We were aware of the extent to which these environmental variables condition the attitudes, perceptions, and behaviors of the individual and, at the same time, mediate and determine the alternatives, opportunities, and constraints that constitute the parameters of the situation in which the individual can act.

Despite the fact that there has been very little research on black female teenagers, policies and programs have been developed based on some untested assumptions and generalizations of doubtful applicability.[5] For example, the issue of motivation has been highlighted while little attention has been paid to the impact of dysfunctional educational and training systems. At the same time that questionable associations are made between family structure and socioeconomic status and unemployment, there has been a preoccupation with the single critical variable, which inevitably leads to simplistic solutions.

Generalizations have been made about this population as a subgroup of ghetto residents and about the prevalence of stereotypes. The studies of Jeffers and Lewis, however, shed light on the extent of variation among poor families despite the fact that they share the same socioeconomic profile and family structure.[6] Herzog has raised important questions about the way in which stereotypes or half-truths obscure significant individual variations and lead to distorted conclusions.[7]

We believed that we would need to review and modify current assumptions and reexamine those generalizations that did not reflect inputs from field experiences. We felt that it was imperative to resist the pressure to reach definitive, simple answers to complex questions. We were committed to finding out what we needed to learn with the commensurate responsibility to redefine old questions and ask appropriate new ones.

In 1964, Harlem Youth Opportunities Unlimited (HARYOU) produced a monumental study on the Central Harlem community, *Youth in the Ghetto*. Every aspect of life in the ghetto was explored, and powerlessness proved to be the unrelenting theme of each. The employment difficulties of black youth were then described as social dynamite:

> Twice as many young Negro men in the labor force, as compared to their white counterparts, were without jobs. For the girls, the gap was even greater—nearly two and one-half times the unemployment rate for white girls in the labor force.[8]

HARYOU called for a comprehensive youth program to address the three main areas contributing to the pathology of the community: education, employment, and family life. Specifically, in terms of employment, they proposed the Employment and Occupational Training Program, which would equip each participant with marketable job skills and, where necessary, remedial education.

A comparison of the lists of social agencies serving Central Harlem then and now shows some new names but, basically, no relief from inadequacy. A comparison of the black teenage unemployment then and now is bleak;

unemployment is worse in absolute terms as well as in terms relative to the rate for white teenagers. Black teenagers continued to suffer due to a lack of quality education and training. Central Harlem is not a stranger to social research; however, it does appear a stranger to results.

The findings of this study are reported in three chapters. Chapter 4 discusses the major modifications that had to be made in the research strategy in order for us to collect data. Chapter 5 treats the study groups and their communities. The employment problems of black teenage females are highlighted in chapter 6.

Throughout the study we were concerned with policy options. Some of our recommendations are highlighted in chapter 2, "Summary and Recommendations."

A bibliography of pertinent books and articles is appended to the study.

4

The Research Strategy

Modification of Original Field Strategy

This chapter reports on the methods and techniques developed and utilized in the data collection, describes the study processes, and discusses the original research plan and subsequent considerations that led to a modified research strategy. Initially, we had proposed to collect the basic data on unemployment among a sample of black female teenagers through the use of structured and unstructured interviews, supplemented by life histories from selected respondents. We were particularly interested in their perceptions of: the characteristics and availability of work, the desirability of work, and job expectations and opportunities. One hundred young females, sixteen to nineteen years old, out of school and not working, were to be selected from the two urban poverty neighborhoods of Central Harlem and Bedford-Stuyvesant.

In the early stages of the field research, it became clear that this procedure was impracticable:

1. Despite the acceptance of MARC as a research-action organization, with a concern for the problems of the poor and minority community, it was recognized that the hostility and resistance of a significant sector of the black community toward research and surveys would extend to the project. This fact was taken into account in planning contacts with community agencies, as well as with the target population. Letters were not used to set up site visits, and in most instances, unscheduled visits to neighborhood programs were more productive. Even with these precautions, however, some data on program utilization and effectiveness proved unobtainable because of the politics of funding and community control. See our discussion of visits to job referral agencies.

2. The target population was not accessible through community recreational or athletic centers, nor through other community and public places, since they had no discernible pattern of congregating in groups. During the first two months of the project, the field staff of three young, black social workers toured the two study communities (day and night) to observe the physical and social context in which the study population lived; identified community agencies and health and welfare facilities; and noted where black teenage females congregated, what their patterns of activities were, and the extent to which they utilized community recreation and athletic centers.

15

Specific information from preliminary field work is reported in chapter 5, "The Study Groups and Their Communities."

3. Employment, training, and referral centers did not provide a pool of young females from which to draw a study group of one hundred. More than forty agencies (the majority located in the study communities) offering either training, preplacement, employment, or social services to youth were visited during the early months of the project. Several complex and interrelated factors accounted for the failure of the agencies to provide interviewees for the study:

a. Agencies were not programmed or staffed to establish individualized relationships with the teenagers.
b. In many instances, young black females were "pushed" and/or screened out of programs because of the priority given by both governmental agencies and civil rights organizations to the unemployment problem of black males.
c. The thrust of federal programs for women was to remove AFDC mothers from the public assistance rolls.
d. There was a scarcity of jobs.
e. As a result of the above factors, the young black females had a negative hostile perception of the centers.

As the staff explored the Harlem and Brooklyn communities, new criteria for the study were developed based on more precise knowledge of the community and the target population. The teenage network emerged as the most effective technique for reaching the study group. A secretary who had been assigned to the project greatly facilitated our ability to establish and maintain contact with a core of black teenage females in Central Harlem. The secretary shared many of the same family characteristics and community experiences of members of our target population. In addition, she had successfully utilized some of the newer job-training programs to acquire secretarial skills. She helped recruit young black females from her community, assisted these girls with a variety of problems (employment, family, educational), served as a role model, and helped to explain the study and objectives to the group. (See Figure 4-1.)

Formation of Harlem Teenage Network

The small core of twelve black teenagers recruited in Harlem served as resource assistants on the project. Their functions were to help recruit the subjects to be interviewed from their home community, and to serve as a pilot or study group reflecting in miniature the salient attitudes and behaviors of the

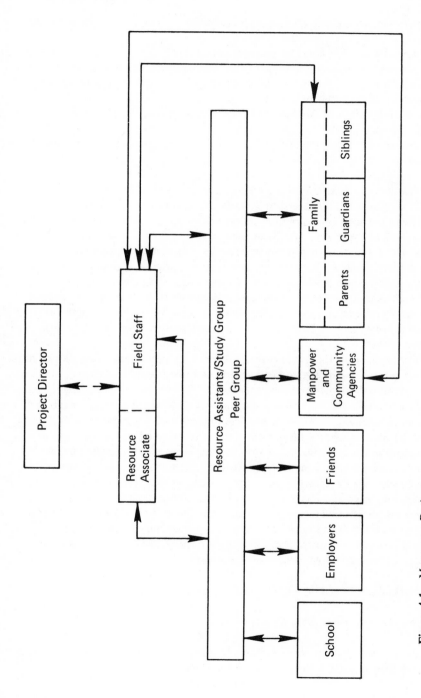

Figure 4-1. Manpower Project

larger sample. The resource assistants assisted the staff in a variety of ways to:

1. contact and interact with the target population;
2. increase the staff's knowledge of the black teenage female population, and the sociopsychological and attitudinal factors affecting their educational and employment situation;
3. gain insight into young black females' perceptions of the characteristics, availability, and alternatives to work; and
4. demonstrate the issues and techniques involved in group formation and development.

The resource assistants also were asked to (1) relate their perceptions of agency services to the staff and to identify the gaps in stated policies and services; (2) to seek jobs in public and private employment and to report these experiences to the group; and (3) to assist in the design of the survey instrument. The resource assistants worked for the project and in that capacity were compensated $5.00 for each weekly group session attended, and at a rate of $2.50 per hour, plus expenses, for assignments related to the job hunt. Thus, at an early stage, the girls were engaged in quasi-work activities which required them to complete assignments, keep schedules, and to become oriented to certain routines such as Thursday night group meetings. (See detailed discussions in chapter 5.)

The response of the initial core of resource assistants and the development of a cohesive group with regular participation by most members meeting in weekly group sessions demonstrated the potential of this method for providing substantive data as well as its validity as a technique for studying the multiple interacting factors related to labor force participation of black teenaged females. Pretesting of the questionnaire with the study group revealed a basic antagonism of this population to the interview technique structured by a formal questionnaire.

For these reasons, a modified research strategy was adopted. Priority was given to enlisting the target population through peer group contacts; the group sessions were used as a major source of data collection, and the technique of participant observer was exploited in an effort to enter into the life space of the study population. The emergence of the group session as the primary research instrument and the revealed shortcomings of a questionnaire were significant findings of the first three months of the project.

Methods and Techniques of Data Collection

Small Group Participant Observation

In our investigation of the factors affecting the perception and involvement of black teenage girls in the world of work, the field staff interacted with the

Harlem and Brooklyn study groups, their individual members, their families, and their peers in a number of different ways. By far the single most important procedure was the group session. Begun as an exploratory method to identify the variety and relative importance of factors influencing employment attitudes and behavior, this method soon dominated all others in importance and data yielded. When other scheduled methods failed, it alone proved continuously successful in obtaining the participation, provoking the thought, and stimulating the interest of both study groups, thus insuring a constant flow of data on attitudes, perceptions, community, family, and friends.

The peer group was used to facilitate the field staff's entry into the life space of the study population. The group provided new sources of data and insight into the configuration of interacting factors which affect the attitudes, responses, and work behaviors of black teenage females seeking jobs. The weekly group sessions were an effective technique for sharpening conceptual issues with respect to the kinds of problems posed to young black females and the ways in which they try to solve them. The group provided an opportunity to study in-depth special social behaviors and peer relationships in the context of a task oriented semistructured group session. Base line data about the interplay of a wide range of personal, family, peer group, and community factors and their impact over a period of time were obtained through participant observation in the ongoing life space of these young black females by the field staff team.

Once a week, for approximately two hours, the study groups met informally—the Harlem group at the home of the resource associate (the project secretary), the Brooklyn group at the home of a resource assistant—to discuss the role of the group, self-development and family relations, and peer group relationships. These topics were usually preplanned by staff and study groups at the preceding weekly meeting. Guided by these plans, each group session, nevertheless, remained flexible, easily accommodating topics of particular interest arising during the meeting.

The job hunt and related interview and job experiences were often topics of discussion during group sessions. Sometimes community or family problems that were more immediately pressing or more universal were brought up. For example, when a girl discussed a suspicious job offer—a man offered her bookkeeping training and experience, then paid her more than the agreed upon wage and suggested they take a weekend trip—other girls discussed similar propositions and other nonjob situations involving sexual abuse and exploitation.

Beside their most obvious function as a rich source of data, these group sessions served as a vehicle for developing rapport between the field staff and the Harlem and Brooklyn core groups. Functioning as participant-observers, taking on the roles of group members, yet maintaining their research objective, the field staff gradually assuaged the suspicions of the study groups and won their acceptance. This produced an atmosphere conducive to spontaneous, unguarded conversation in which attitudes, values, and life situations were freely discussed. Once this relaxed atmosphere and ease of conversation prevailed, the staff gradually decreased its participation in order that the members of the study groups could take on increasing responsibility for their group. It was in this setting that the special activities (to be discussed later in this section) were initiated. Interesting topics led to suggestions that they be pursued by the group beyond the weekly sessions. Field trips were planned, and experts were invited to lecture on subjects of special interest to the group. Role playing provided an excellent vehicle for focusing on personal, employment, and family problems. These techniques arising from the group session furnished supplementary data, as well as a check on insights gained during the group sessions.

The continuing series of group meetings allowed the participant-observers to become responsive to the moods and special needs of individual group members, thus preventing potential sources of disruption and cushioning the possible negative impact of the group on an individual member under duress. The continuous sessions also gave the staff the opportunity to single out recurring themes. The resource assistants and staff members were at all times conscious of the employment focus of the project. Job hunts were introduced during the first month of the project. Yet it became clear at the first meeting that employment could only be discussed along with other issues and institutions that affect the lives of these young women. Often the major themes were schools, family problems, and peer relationships.

A taped record was made of each group session, and detailed staff notes supplemented these materials. In conjunction with the group meetings, staff meetings were held twice weekly. One meeting was scheduled shortly before the group session to review tapes and staff notes of the sessions; to share pertinent information, and to project the issues, objectives, format, and staff roles for the upcoming meeting. The second meeting was held on the morning following the group session to evaluate the session; to identify and review the significant data which had emerged, and to consider the implications for future group sessions and individual contacts.

The resource assistants took very seriously their responsibility to attend the group meetings regularly and to participate actively. They were extremely critical of any member who failed in these obligations. Few of the resource assistants had previously participated in formal or informal groups—nor dervied any satisfactions from group experiences.

Activities included role playing focused on personal and family problems, a group discussion of an autobiography of a southern black teenager, a session on sex education and family planning led by a black male staff member from Planned Parenthood; and recruiting of unemployed teenagers for the sample survey.

The group became one of the significant dimensions of each member's life space. In a number of instances the families were aware of the group's meaning

to the teenager. The project experience demonstrated that poor black teenagers
can be motivated to participate in an ongoing group and can derive meaningful
individual satisfactions from this experience.

The success of the staff in forming a viable group of twelve black teenage
females in Harlem and six in Bedford-Stuyvesant was due to: (1) the confidence
the teenagers had in the field staff; (2) the appropriateness and accessibility of
the setting for the group meetings; black teenagers have generally "put down"
the traditional agency settings such as the YWCA or after-school community
centers; and (3) the opportunity members of the group were given to share in
the formulation of the objectives, program, and group processes themselves.

The field staff operating as a team was an important component of the
process. The criteria for the field staff were based on knowledge of the community, the target population, and the research objectives. The three members of the field staff were young black females. Two of them had social
work experience and had also worked as interviewers with large public opinion
survey organizations. The third person had worked in training and personnel
with a large insurance firm which hired young females, many of them black.
Each member of the field staff had to bridge the social distance between
herself and the study population.

The acceptance of staff members by the Harlem group was by no means
automatic. Each staff member's dress, vocabulary, mannerisms, and associates
were subject to close scrutiny. Late in August, the group had to adapt to a
change in staff; one staff member left the project in order to go to graduate
school, and a summer intern who participated in field activities returned
to college in her home state of Mississippi. A new staff member, a social
worker who had traveled and studied in Africa, began attending sessions.
By mid-September the group members had "checked out" the staff and
generally agreed that staff were "all right."

The field staff members were a more cohesive and self-confident team
when the Brooklyn group was formed and gained access to the community
without the introduction by a resource associate. Nevertheless, resource
assistants observed them with the same great interest. There was evidence
that resource assistants began to use field staff as role models, expressing
an active interest in the staff's families, educational backgrounds, and social
activities.

The resource associate also added an important dimension to the investigation. The activities of the resource associate were designed to complement
and support these group sessions with more personal and individualized
attention to each member of the group. Such interactions on a one-to-one
level in the teenager's natural setting were expected to involve more spon-
taneity of behavior, greater emotional intensity, a wider spectrum of behaviors,
and a relationship of longer duration than the group session, whose merits
will be discussed later in this section.

The crucial role of the resource associate is best illustrated by the following list of her activities:

1. filling out forms and applications for jobs, assistance, school, etc.;
2. explaining correspondence from the Department of Social Services, government agencies, and businesses;
3. advising on family problems;
4. tutoring and studying;
5. preventing crises—for example, locating a subject who disappeared from her home;
6. providing information about community resources;
7. serving as a role model;
8. clarifying group projects and decisions; and
9. being available for teenage "rapping" (informal talks).

The importance of this role was further realized with efforts to establish the Brooklyn study group. Difficulties not encountered with the Harlem study group ensued when a parallel resource associate indigenous to the Brooklyn community could not be located. Except for this difference, the same staff serviced both the Harlem and Brooklyn study groups.

The group meetings were generally informal, and there was no discussion leader as such. The meetings provided an intimate kind of situational analysis, since *every* member of the group was forced to relate to every other member with great personal candor. Under the informal arrangements of the group meetings it was possible for the staff to record and analyze the random and evolutionary process by which the assistants, through their association, became a primary support system for one another in dealing with the larger society as well as with their family units.

By the end of the field activity, each member of the group had demonstrated a potential for active participation despite the wide variation in their personalities, previous experiences, specific motivations, and interests in the group tasks. From September through December the Harlem group took increasing responsibility for carrying out their role and functions for the project. They agreed to be subjects and were interested in recruiting additional study subjects for the questionnaire. Several sessions were devoted to pretesting and revising the questionnaire. The decision to abandon the questionnaire as an effective way of collecting data could be undertaken only because the girls accepted the obligation of the project to provide data. They expressed willingness to be subjects and cooperated with the field staff's use of individual and family interviews as important data collection techniques.

Survey Instrument

As the field staff learned more about the experiences of the young black

females in their families, peer groups, schools, and communities, it became clear
that simple questioning of this target population would not yield valid and
reliable data. We attempted to design an instrument that would measure those
variables (peer group relations, family interaction patterns, level of aspirations,
etc.) in a black unemployed teenager's life space which impinged upon her
world of work.

Pretesting the questionnaire with individual subjects and group discussions
gave us insight into some of the difficulties of collecting information on this
particular population. The group's resentment, hostility, and suspicion aroused
by the questionnaire indicated their unwillingness and/or inability to give information in this manner. Many simple questions evoked emotional reactions of
blocking or denial. We learned that there was wide variation in the meaning of
even the most common words; negative connotations were attached to questions often because of their associations with the previous experiences of the
girls.

It was not possible to get a reliable answer to many questions. For example,
even though a resource assistant had not worked for several weeks and probably
could not return to the job, she considered herself employed until she decided
one day that she was no longer interested in the job. A Brooklyn resource
assistant did not reveal that she was married since she was still living at home.
Some resource assistants considered themselves in school because they had
registered at the beginning of the semester, even though they did not attend
classes.

Certain responses and behaviors could only be understood by probing to
secure cross-sectional data about the varied contributing factors. For example,
probing of one resource assistant's matter-of-fact announcement that she was
quitting her job revealed: (1) anger and disgust about her supervisor's sexual
advances, (2) cynicism about the community's value system and priorities
since her brother did nothing to earn his weekly Neighborhood Youth Corps
check, (3) resentment of her parents lenient attitude toward her brother, and
(4) boredom with a routine low-skill job. Her reaction resulted from the
simultaneous surfacing of several significant issues. This would have been
missed in a simple questionnaire administered by an interviewer who was
unfamiliar with the many salient factors impinging on her employment status.
Probing of cross-sectional data permits one to analyze the range of base line
data and specific factors that create stressful situations or evoke responses
and behaviors that cannot be fully understood.

Comments Made by Harlem Resource
Assistants on the Questionnaire

Harlem resource assistants objected to questions on the questionnaire
which appeared to be: too personal and/or offensive; irrelevant to the stated

purpose of the questionnaire; and not easily understood (the usage of words unfamiliar to them) or too ambiguous.

Questions which drew the most controversy and the strongest rejection on the part of the resource assistants were those which dealt with family and boyfriends. These questions were perceived by the girls to be too personal.

In addition, the resource assistants did not wish to have their friends who might be recruited for the larger survey asked such prying questions. They feared that these friends would then look upon them suspiciously.

Examples:

Question: Name of persons living with you and their relationship to you?
Reaction: Suppose you're not living with your people, or suppose you have
              somebody living with you who isn't related—you don't want
              to tell somebody that you don't know them. That's getting into
              your business. So what they'll do is just lie, and if they do that,
              why ask the question?

Question: Are any of these family members working? Where? What type
              of job?
Reactions: Suppose you say they're not working, then they think you're
              on welfare.
              Some people don't know where people in their family work.
              Because people in my family don't work doesn't mean that I
              won't work, anyway.

Question: Do you have a boyfriend?
Reaction: It's nobody's business. Besides, what girl is going to say she
              doesn't have a boyfriend?

Question: Does your boyfriend/husband help support you?
Reaction: If you have a baby or something, you don't want to say that he
              doesn't give you anything.

The questions considered irrelevant to the stated purpose of the questionnaire (employment) were those which dealt with peer group relationships. The resource assistants tended to feel that friends did not influence them to work or not to work.

Examples:

Question: Do you know any girls who use drugs? Do you think using drugs
              keeps them from working?
Reactions: Some girls won't want to answer that because then the person
              [interviewer] will think she does, too, and everybody knows
              somebody who uses drugs.
              Aspirin is a drug.

Question: Do your friends out of school have jobs?
Reaction: That has nothing to do with me working, cause my friends work
              don't mean that I have to work. I can get money in the street.

Questions objected to due to the usage of words unfamiliar to them primarily called for definitions of terms frequently used in the world of work. The resource assistants had difficulty in defining the terms, but often stated that they had an idea of what the term meant. The three questions that required definitions were often answered with a question-statement response—"That has something to do with jobs, right?"

Examples:

Questions: What is meant by fringe benefits?
              What is overtime pay?
              What is the job of a supervisor?
Reaction: You feel bad when you don't even know what they're asking.

Question: Do community agencies offer good jobs?
Reaction: A lot of people don't know what community agencies are. I
              know because we talked about it. If you don't know what they
              are, then you can't say they offer good jobs or not.

The resource assistants found other questions to be ambiguous.

Question: Do you have any health problems that might keep you from
              finding or keeping a job? What are they?
Reaction: Well, using drugs is a health problem. Is that what you mean?

Even though the plan to interview one-hundred girls in the two urban poverty neighborhoods was abandoned, the Harlem group felt obliged to work on another version of the questionnaire for some of their acquaintances who had been told about the project. Four girls were recruited and interviewed by the Harlem resource assistants. There was no objection to these sessions being taped. However, the interviewees asked, "If you are not getting us jobs or new services (such as day care), then why must we be interviewed?" Two of the respondents indicated that they wanted to work but could not find babysitters.

Thus, from October through February, the Harlem resource assistants pretested the instrument, recruited several girls for the larger survey, but, more importantly, interacted with staff and other unemployed black teenagers on their personal and environmental problems as they were related to employment. The motto selected for the jobs section of their instrument was: "So Get A Job, Be Somebody—Because You Are."

The decision to abandon the questionnaire took all of these facts into consideration. The loss, if any, represented no real loss of information, for the group session in conjunction with other activities provided indirectly what the questionnaire failed to yield directly. Constructive patterns of interaction could not have resulted from the administration of a questionnaire. The process of developing an instrument served to facilitate the participant observation process. In addition to this advantage, the group sessions proved fertile ground for the evolvement and refinement of other methods of data collection which collectively formed a dynamic, creative research process. These methods were scheduled individual interviews in the homes of the resource assistants, unscheduled interviews in several places, and special activities.

Scheduled Interviews of Assistants and Their Families

Partly in lieu of the questionnaire interview, scheduled individual interviews were adopted to obtain specific and basic background data on each member of the Harlem and Brooklyn study groups. Structured only in barest outline by topics to be broached during conversation, the interview maintained the informal atmosphere that had become the signature of the group session.

The interviews were conducted in either the home of the resource assistant, the home where weekly group sessions were held, or at MARC. For some resource assistants, more than one interview was scheduled. When family members or friends were present during the interview, this afforded the staff person an opportunity to acquaint them with the project. This practice secured still another entry into the resource assistant's life space and provided supplementary data to qualify and aid in interpreting the data.

Aside from the group meetings, unscheduled contacts became the most important occasion for interaction with the assistants. Unscheduled contacts between resource assistants and staff occurred in several ways. Often resource assistants would come early to the group session, hoping for an opportunity to talk with a staff member. Sometimes group members would just "appear" at the MARC office; only a few preceded these visits with a telephone call. Most frequently, however, the resource assistants would seek out the resource associate to talk over their problems. The subject to these meetings usually had to do with personal crises or problems in filling out forms for job applications or applications for training programs. Random street contacts within the neighborhood reinforced the responsiveness and group identification of the assistants.

Special Activities

On the basis of their growing familiarity with black teenaged girls, the field staff anticipated and was therefore prepared when the resource assistants indicated an interest in social activities beyond the group session. These unstructured situations provided the staff with an opportunity to participate in situations where the authority element—which was to an extent inherent in the formal group sessions—was absent. Special activities of the Harlem study group included: visits to the Schomburg Library, a local library with an outstanding collection of black literature; an exhibition of works by black artists; a group theater party and a play by a black playwright. One activity co-sponsored by the Harlem and Brooklyn study groups, a game-birthday party, was held at the MARC office.

Conclusion

The staff found the participant-observer technique with the peer group to be the most effective way to learn about the critical areas of interaction between the unemployed black teenage females and the world of work.

After one lengthy group session where several girls aired personal problems, the staff observer noted, "Apparently, rap sessions allow the group to talk about problems and possible solutions without the feeling that they, specifically, are being exposed." When "rapping," one girl's problem will prompt others to talk about their problems, feelings, and experiences. Much of the data that is difficult, if not impossible, to get at through direct questioning is freely discussed and receives group support in "rapping" sessions.

5

The Study Groups and Their Communities

Both Harlem and Bedford-Stuyvesant are low-income, predominantly black communities with a sizable number of the residents receiving welfare assistance. In 1971 more than 50 percent of the residents of Bedford-Stuyvesant and 30 to 40 percent of the residents of Central Harlem received welfare.[1] Jobs, education, and drugs are a constant source of difficulty in these major poverty areas. Table 5-1 compares the labor force status of black teenage females for the United States, New York City, and the low-income areas in which the members of the study group resided. During 1970–71, the unemployment rate among black female teenagers in the poverty areas of New York City was 32.7 percent as compared with a national rate of 35.5 percent.[2]

In the Harlem low-income tracts one-fifth of the five thousand sixteen-to-nineteen-year-old black females were in the labor force, but they were mainly the eighteen-to-nineteen-year-olds who were not enrolled in school. In the low-income areas of Bedford-Stuyvesant less than a fifth of the twelve thousand sixteen-to-nineteen-year-old black females were in the labor force, and the older nonstudents accounted for almost two-thirds of these labor force participants. Since those not enrolled in school made up such a large proportion of the unemployed black teenage work force in both Harlem and Bedford-Stuyvesant, the high rates of unemployment reflected the adversities of an out-of-school population rather than seasonal activities of students. (See table 5-2). This section will examine the New York City labor market, activities of the study groups, and briefly describe three aspects of the communities in which these young females lived: referral and training agencies, educational facilities, and the drug problem.

New York City Labor Market

The difficulties imposed on black adult workers is important in discussing the employment problems of young black workers. The employment hardships experienced by the parents and guardians of black adolescents negatively affect the youths' lives and future prospects for the world of work. In the New York labor market of more than three million persons, nonwhites account for one-fifth of the workers. The overall unemployment rate in New York City was 6.7 percent in 1971 as compared with 7.8 percent for black workers.[3] However, the unemployment rate of blacks in the major poverty areas of New York—Central

29

Table 5-1
Black Teenage Females, 16-19 Years Old, 1970

	United States[a]	Low Income Areas[b] (in thousands)					
		United States	New York City	Manhattan	Manhattan Area I	Brooklyn	Brooklyn Area II
Noninstitutional Population	953,813	272.0	35.2	7.1	4.6	17.6	12.5
Civilian Labor Force	240,949	100.0	7.3	1.6	0.9	3.0	2.1
Employed[c]	191,025	62.0	4.9	1.0	0.7	2.2	1.6
Unemployed	49,924	38.0	2.4	0.6	0.2	0.8	0.5
Unemployment rate	20.7%	37.9%	32.9%	37.6%	24.6%	26.0%	24.4%
Not in Labor Force[d]	711,561	172.0	27.9	5.5	3.7	14.6	10.4

[a]Census of Population: 1970, *Negro Population*, Subject Report PC(2)-1B, p. 71.

[b]Census of Population: 1970, *Employment Profiles of Selected Low Income Areas*, Report PHC (3)-1, 2, 4, 5, 7, 9.

[c]Low-income figures derived; difference between unemployed and civilian labor force.

[d]Low-income figures derived; difference between population and civilian labor force.

Table 5-2
Black Teenage Females in Harlem and Brooklyn[a]
(Low-Income Areas)

Age	Popula- tion	Enrolled in School	Labor Force		Unemployed	
			Student	Nonstudent	Student	Nonstudent
Harlem						
16-17	2,519	2,162	64	192		
18-19	2,077	968	98	593		
Total	4,596	3,130	162	785	66	167
Bedford-Stuyvesant						
16-17	6,310	5,761	91	137		
18-19	6,183	3,385	503	1,330		
Total	12,493	9,146	594	1,467	91	412

[a]Census of Population: 1970, *Employment Profiles of Selected Low Income Areas,* Reports 5 and 9.

Harlem, East Harlem, the South Bronx, and Bedford-Stuyvesant—was substantially higher. In low-income area Number I of Manhattan, black males experienced unemployment rates of 9.2 percent and black women 5.6 percent; the unemployment rate for black males and females living in the low-income Survey Area II of Brooklyn was 8.1 percent and 7.0 percent, respectively.

Sharp differences between black/white and nonpoverty/poverty area residents existed prior to the downswing of the economy. In the twelve-month period ending June 1969, the unemployment rate for New York City's major poverty areas was 2.1 times that for the New York metropolitan area. The gaps were only continued during the recession.

In 1971, New York City lost 130,000 payroll jobs, with most of the decline in factory employment. Since World War II, the decline in factory employment has been significant.[4] A study conducted by the New York City Planning Commission predicts that two-thirds of the manufacturing companies and 55 percent of the jobs that are likely to move out of the city annually will move from Manhattan. The comparative figures for Brooklyn were 9.3 percent of the companies and 25.3 percent of the jobs.[5] Many of the factories leaving the city are relocating outside of the metropolitan area. In 1966 it was calculated that it could cost a Harlem resident $40 per month for public transportation to a job site in Westchester County, Staten Island, or Long Island—$50 a month for a Bedford-Stuyvesant resident.[6] Since that time, transit fares have increased several times.

Along with the decline of factory work there has been a steady flow of unskilled workers with limited employment mobility into the city's labor pool. Blacks are overrepresented in blue-collar jobs, mainly at the operative (low-skill) level. According to poverty area data, during the period July 1968 to June 1969, the occupational distribution of workers living in New York City ghettos was 40 percent in blue-collar jobs.[7] A recent study of projected changes in occupational employment in New York City reveals that by 1980 white-collar occupations will account for 71 percent of all jobs to be filled.[8]

Manpower researchers have become increasingly concerned about the number and characteristics of nonparticipants in the labor force. In the poverty areas of New York City overall labor force participation rates among blacks were 73.1 percent of civilian noninstitutionalized men and 49.5 percent of women. Among teenagers (aged sixteen to nineteen labor force participation is much greater for blacks (49 percent of males, 42 percent of females) than for white teenagers (36 percent of white males, 39 percent of females).[9] School attendance is frequently a reason for nonparticipation—although many young people who are in school are also working, looking, or interested in jobs. When young in-school people work it is usually to supplement family income or to provide spending money for themselves.

In New York City's poverty neighborhoods, 49,000, or nearly two-fifths, of all female nonparticipants sixteen and over said that they were not working or looking for work because of family responsibilities. This group did not include the 45,000 who keep house but did not cite this responsibility as their major reason for not working. This suggests that if the jobs available were structured differently (for example, different hours, different locations) or if other means existed for carrying out the household responsibilities, many more women would become more active participants in the labor market. The lack of day care facilities was cited by 7000 women as a barrier to entering the work world. Of these, 4100 stated that they would use day care facilities if available; 1100 said that they might use them. The day care problems for mothers in the target area, Central Harlem and Bedford-Stuyvesant, are discussed later.

In 1970 unemployment in all standard metropolitan statistical areas averaged 8.3 percent for blacks and 4.9 percent for whites. The changing characteristics of urban labor markets, suburbanization of jobs, and decline in manufacturing activity have reduced employment opportunities for workers confined to central city locations. Even when jobs are available in these areas, the poor are employed mainly in secondary labor markets in jobs that are less attractive than those offered by the primary labor market. The jobs in the secondary sector tend to involve low wages, poor working conditions, considerable variety in employment, harsh and often arbitrary discipline, and little opportunity to advance.[10]   Black workers, in addition, have frequently experienced the most severe kinds of employment discrimination.

In 1970 the median annual earnings of year-round, full-time workers was $4908 for black females and $6124 for black males for the Harlem community. The income gap was doubled for those black families headed by females as compared with those headed by males. Thirty-seven percent of all black families headed by females had incomes below the poverty level as compared with 16 percent for black families headed by males.

In the Bedford-Stuyvesant community 40 percent of black families headed by females were below the poverty level. Median annual earnings of year-round, full-time workers was $5185 and $6628 for black females and males, respectively. The income gap between black families headed by females and those headed by males was $3818. These black families in low-income areas were more likely to fall below the poverty level of existence and the children in these families are deprived at an early age of minimum requirements for a decent standard of living.

This is the situation that faces the families of young, poor, black females. The parents and other adults with whom they have contact have not, as a group, fared well in the labor market. Regardless of the expectations and aspirations they have for their children, these parents probably have difficulty in presenting enviable images of working adults.

Comparison of the Study Groups and Their Communities

The twelve Harlem resource assistants held thirty-seven intensive group sessions over a ten-month period (July 1970 to April 1971), and the smaller Brooklyn core group of six met over four months. (See tables 5-3 and 5-4.) Despite the fact that the entire study group came from a fairly narrow economic, social, and educational range, there was wide variation in their family characteristics, current work or school attitudes, peer group relationships, and other attributes. The majority of the Harlem assistants came from families who were second- and third-generation New Yorkers with immediate family ties and experience from this area. The Brooklyn assistants represented more recent family migration to New York, usually from southern states; they were more reserved and more mature in their behavior and in their manner of addressing problems. The Brooklyn group came from larger families and seemed to have closer family ties.

The project tapes, interviews, and discussions show that these black teenage females whose families are poor residents of an urban ghetto are not a homogeneous group despite the similarity of their surface characteristics. In this small sample there were varied patterns of family structure. The parents included alcoholics and the mentally ill, the disorganized and the hard-working upwardly mobile. Some were actively concerned about their children, and others were defeated and apathetic. In some homes poverty and deprivation stalked, while in others the effects of poverty were offset by the coping strengths of the parents or other significant family members. One observation that was common to most families during the ten months of observation was that there is a precarious balance at best which is disturbed by recurrent practical or personal crises.

The Central Harlem group included members with a wide range of educational achievement extending from a junior high school dropout to a first-year college student. Some members of the group were involved with drugs, but the study population was not among the addicts who have left home and found their own drug culture. In fact, they were not part of any well-established youth network. The group included several unmarried mothers, but there was little evidence to support the views that illegitimacy is a way of life and that the value of marriage is not appreciated. Almost all of the girls, whether or not they had children, considered a lasting marriage a desirable goal.

We were not able to establish the expected associations between the complex of factors that we began to identify and examine. One could not distinguish between those resource assistants with families who received public assistance and those with one or more working parents, whether we examined their work-related attitudes or the level of living. In some families, as in all American families, the efforts of upwardly mobile, highly active parents were often counterproductive, either for intrapersonal reasons or because the parents could not offset the community pressures. The married resource assistants continued to live with their families; young single members lived apart from their families.

The Harlem Group

The Harlem group was the first to be constituted. Because of the general feeling that "research never helps the community," it was essential that the project simultaneously provide short-term service to the participant members from the community and gather the required data on black female teenagers' perceptions of and adjustments to unemployment and potential opportunities to enter the work force.

At the time of the first contact, the girls were told that their help was needed in order to try and improve the employment situation for themselves and other minority workers who had experienced unemployment or were trapped in dead-end jobs. Some of the girls periodically asked for assistance in finding jobs; others sought advice and assistance with personal family problems. Dealing with these requests for exchange of service was essential to building confidence in the staff and lending credibility to the sponsoring organization.

A core of twelve black young females was recruited from the Central Harlem community (135th to 148 Streets) and Morningside Heights (116th to 125th Streets)—areas described by the participants as "junkies' paradise" within the general Harlem community (bounded by Broadway or Amsterdam Avenues on the west and the East River on the east, and 110th Street on the south and 150th Street on the north). The Central Harlem area was slightly smaller than Area I of the Manhattan as defined by the special 1970-71 census survey of low income areas.

Nine of the resource assistants lived within a few blocks walking distance of one another in Central Harlem; the remaining three, one of whom moved to the Bronx while a group member, used public transportation to attend group meetings. Such proximity made contact among the resource assistants a relatively frequent and natural occurrence. Even though group membership was fixed at twelve, friends and peers of the members frequently attended sessions and participated in discussions.

Table 5-3 shows the characteristics of the twelve Harlem participants compiled from the information given by the girls about themselves. When the group was formed all of the girls were single; four were school dropouts, four had children, seven were from families where some assistance was received from the Department of Social Services, and five were from families where adult members were employed. Even the detailed profiles for each member of the Harlem group cannot adequately reflect the attitudes, responses, and behaviors of black teenage females with respect to peer relationships, family factors, employment status, community pressures, and the recurring harsh crises that confront the poor black ghetto resident. Nor do these profiles sufficiently illuminate the dynamics of the lives of these young women, the existence of frequent changes in fact and perception that are reflected in the girls' comments about themselves.

When Department of Labor representatives conducted an on-site visit in March 1971, three members of the Harlem group had an opportunity to talk to them. They related their group experiences, expressed enthusiasm about the project, and requested funds to be continued. In doing so, they demonstrated their newly developed capability to maneuver in a businesslike situation. The Harlem group decided to meet regularly after the termination of the project and hopes to be able to participate in existing programs which might strengthen their personal growth. When asked what had the group meant to them, two responses were:

"It's made me realize that I need to go back to school."

"The group has helped me by giving me someone, somewhere to talk about my problems."

The Brooklyn Group

Recruiting a Bedford-Stuyvesant core group of resource assistants was more difficult than establishing the Harlem group. There was no indigenous community

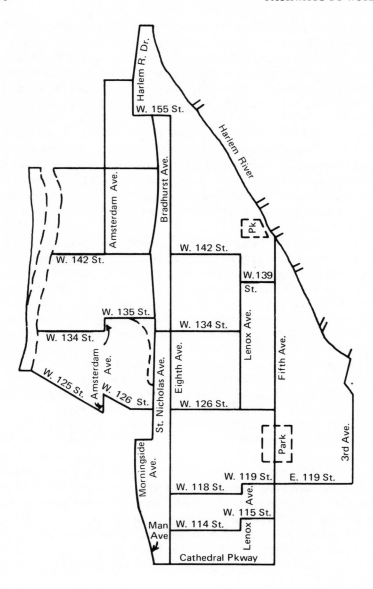

Source: Department of City Planning, City of New York

Figure 5-1: Central Harlem: Survey Area

Table 5-3
Harlem Study Group

1H   Eighteen; one daughter; (married January 1971; lives with daughter and husband); high school dropout; enrolled at New York Adult Training Center; previous work experience.

2H   Seventeen; no children; single; lives with mother and substitute father; twelfth-grade College Bound Program—has been accepted at Hunter College; previous work experience, presently not working.

3H   Eighteen; no children; single; lives with mother and sister; high school graduate, June 1970; presently student at Bronx Community College; presently not working, previous work experience.

4H   Eighteen; one daughter; single; lives with mother and brothers; high school dropout, ninth grade; awaiting entrance to training program; previous work experience, presently not working.

5H   Sixteen; no children; single; living with mother, substitute father and twelve siblings; was placed in Youth Center on several occasions because of parents' neglect and as a result of mother's filing PINS Petition (Person in Need of Supervision); enrolled in eighth grade, but does not attend school regularly; previous work experience.

6H   Fifteen; no children; single; has lived with mother, friends, father, and in Youth Center during nine months of project; enrolled in eighth grade in a junior high school, but does not attend school; not working, no work experience.

7H   Seventeen; no children; single; lives with mother, sister, and brothers; school dropout, ninth grade; enrolled in WIN Program, but does not attend regularly; not working, previous work experience.

8H   Seventeen; one daughter; single; lives with substitute mother, substitute father and a brother; enrolled in tenth grade of high school; previous work experience.

9H   Seventeen; no children; single; lives with mother; enrolled in tenth grade of high school, commercial course; no work experience.

10H   Seventeen; no children; single; living with father, brother, substitute mother and her children; enrolled in eleventh grade at vocational high school; not working, previous work experience.

11H   Seventeen; no children; single; lives with mother, father, siblings; eleventh grade high school, academic course; previous work experience.

12H   Seventeen; one daughter; single; shares apartment with brother (nineteen years old) and girlfriend (nineteen years old); high school dropout after tenth grade; presently not working, previous work experience.

---

member available to introduce staff to the study population. One field staff member was a former Bedford-Stuyvesant resident and was familiar with the Brooklyn area. With the aid of two young women who sought friends and neighbors to participate in the project, a Brooklyn core group of eight was recruited over a six-week period. However, because of jobs and training programs, only six of these girls were participants throughout the project.

There was less time spent on orientation with the Brooklyn group than with the Harlem group. The staff benefited from the Harlem experimental stage. Job hunts were assigned almost immediately.

The experience with the formation of the Brooklyn group demonstrates that it is possible to replicate the peer group formation even when a comparable personnel strategy cannot be implemented (utilization of an indigenous young staff person to make initial contacts and to be available for questions from the study population).

The Brooklyn resource assistants lived in various sections of the Bedford-Stuyvesant community in Central Brooklyn. Bedford-Stuyvesant as used in this study indicates an area in the north-central section of Brooklyn. Major boundary streets are Myrtle Avenue, Broadway, St. Marks Avenue, and Vanderbilt Avenue. (See Figure 5-2). In the bordering areas of Bushwick, Crown Heights, Fort Greene, Williamsburg, East New York, and Brownsville, the proportion of black residents has been increasing. Bedford-Stuyvesant as defined in this report comprises approximately one-half of the low-income area designated as Survey Area II in the 1970-71 Census Employment Survey of Selected Low-Income Areas.

The assistants in the Brooklyn group did not live close to one another for the most part; four of them had known one another, however, prior to the formation of the group. They were well able to communicate readily about conditions in the high schools, hospitals, shopping districts, and entertainment centers of the community; none of them was satisfied with conditions in their immediate neighborhoods.

It was observed that these girls were less concerned about finding their own identities and planning their lives than the Harlem girls. They talked frequently about the difference between life in the South and the North. For most of them some major decision in a young girl's life had already been made—whether or not

Table 5-4
Brooklyn Study Group

1B   Twenty; no children; single; lives with mother and siblings; Bushwick High School graduate, June 1971; not working, no work experience.

2B   Seventeen; no children; single; lives with mother, three sisters and one brother; enrolled in eleventh grade, Canarsie High School; no work experience.

3B   Twenty; no children; married; lives with mother, husband and siblings; received Bushwick High School certificate, June 1970; now taking business and reading skills courses at SUNY Urban Center in Brooklyn; previous work experience.

4B   Eighteen; one son; married; lives with husband; completed eleventh grade at Bushwick High School; previous work experience; discontinued attendance at group meetings to work for temporary employment agency.

5B   Seventeen; one daughter; unmarried; lives with mother and siblings; participated in Young Mother's Program during pregnancy (fall-winter 1970); enrolled in eleventh grade, Wingate High School; no work experience.

6B   Sixteen; one child; married; living with mother, husband, grandmother and uncle; enrolled in tenth grade, Prospect Heights High School; left school after completing J.H.S. 57 to be married (1968); returned to school in 1970; no work experience.

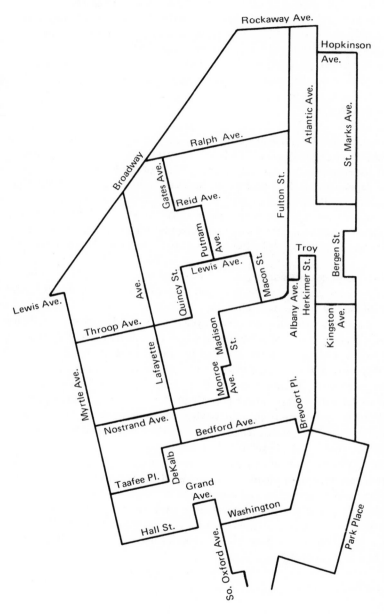

Source: Department of City Planning, City of New York

Figure 5-2. Bedford-Stuyvesant: Survey Area

to complete school; what man they wanted to build their lives with. For those
girls who were either married or had marriage plans, their own career plans
and work status were to be secondary to their mates. They seemed to have set
circles of friends and were in the last stages of obtaining recognition from their
parents as adults. Nevertheless, the girls talked about their problems of growing
up, relating to parents, thinking about occupational goals, and making voca-
tionally oriented choices in school, and planning financial support for their futures.

Family and Friends

The attitudes and behavior of most teenage girls are quite closely tied to
their families or adult guardians with whom they probably live. This held true
for most of the study group, married or single. Nine of the girls in the Harlem
group were dependent on their parents for financial support. Family financial or
housing problems and relationships with parents and siblings were frequently
topics of group session discussions and personal conversation. Of the four girls
who were married, two remained with their husbands in their parents' households.

Girls living at home received parental pressure to use their time in certain
ways:

1. Two resource assistants who did not attend school regularly received
no pressure to go to school or to get jobs, but were responsible for housekeeping
duties and for care of the younger children.

2. The working mother of another resource assistant had tried to facilitate
her children's staying in school or obtaining training elsewhere, and did insist
that her out-of-school, out-of-work daughter do some of the heavy cleaning.
However, this mother was not able to control drug use by her children.

It was common for parents to expect their children to care for younger
children or to delegate to them major household responsibilities. Often they
considered this far more important than having their girls work for low wages.

The stated expectations that parents have for their children are only a part
of the influence that parents have. Children gain certain impressions of the
economic struggle and labor force participation by observing their parents. They
see how their parents obtain income, examine what this means in terms of their
own economic and social status, and observe the effects on their parents
behavior, social life, and emotional well-being. They listen to their parents
direct and indirect comments on their own jobs or the world of work. The
status of black workers in the New York City labor market has been discussed
under the first section of this chapter.

Families Participating in Home Interviews

The seven home visits conducted with families of the Harlem group members revealed a variety of family structures.

1.   In an interview with 1H's mother, opinions about unemployment among black teenage girls and unwed motherhood were expressed. The mother believed that the unemployment of the black teenage girls in the Harlem community was the result of lack of motivation and encouragement rather than availability of jobs. She blamed the parents and the girls and suggested that the girls either complete high school or participate in a skills training program.

1H's mother considered unwed motherhood the deciding factor in whether a teenager should seek employment. In her opinion, once a girl had the responsibility of caring for a child, she no longer had a choice of becoming employed. Welfare was not mentioned as an avenue for support. Marriage was looked upon as the solution, if only partially. The family consisted of five daughters and one son. Three of the daughters, two of their children, and the son lived at home with the mother who was the head of the household.

2.   The family of 4H present for the home interview included the resource assistant's baby, mother, brother, and several friends. The mother indicated approval of her daughter's involvement in the group. The mother indicated that she preferred 4H to return to school or find a job but had not pressured her daughter to do so.

3.   Home visits with 5H and 6H transpired while a minor family crisis was in process. The mother related that her inability to control the two girls had necessitated her taking them to family court. Both the girls and the mother anticipated that the girls would be placed in an institution. The mother indicated that if 5H and 6H were institutionalized, she would know where they were and would not worry about their being "in the streets." The resource assistants implied that they preferred an institutional setting and were not happy in the home under the prevailing conditions with a substitute father living there.

4.   Family of 7H. There were two interviews with 7H's mother, who indicated that her children were her first concern. She mentioned that 7H was often a problem. The mother believed that the reason black teenage girls could not find jobs was because they did not want jobs. She stated that she had never had problems in finding a job.

During the second visit the mother noted that 7H never finished anything. She cited as examples 7H's incomplete high school education, her job at a local grocery, her Job Corps experience, which lasted only two days, and the WIN Program classes in which the resource assistant was enrolled but did not attend regularly. In addition, the mother seemed anxious to discuss her own job training and present job as a psychiatric aide at a hospital.

5.   Resource assistant 8H lives with her brother, her baby, and an unrelated substitute mother and father. The natural mother suffered brain damage and has been periodically hospitalized. However, the natural mother was present during the interview. It was learned during the home contact that the resource assistants's daughter suffered from cerebral palsy.

6.   The home visit to the family of 10H was conducted with the resource assistant's stepmother who spoke of the friction between the resource assistant and herself. 10H shared her home, a private residence recently purchased, with her father, brother, the stepmother, and the stepmother's children by a previous relationship.

7.   The family of 12H lived in a small apartment which she shared with her brother, a drug addict, her girlfriend, the girlfriend's child, and her own daughter. At the time of the visit the resouce assistant was employed but had taken sick leave. She was having difficulty filling out sick leave forms for her job. 12H had to telephone her office, but there was no telephone in the apartment. She indicated that it was difficult to carry her baby to the nearest public telephone. Therefore, she had not made the call. During the remainder of the home visit, staff members encouraged the resource assistant to call immediately.

Friends

In addition to the twenty resource assistants, the field staff met with thirty-four other young women who fell within the definition of the study group. These young women were group session visitors, special activity participants, or questionnaire respondents. There were fourteen visitors, male and female, to the Harlem group sessions. All but one of these were in the same age group as the resource assistants, all were from the same residential environment. A brief description of each visitor follows:

1.   Female, age nineteen, was a roommate of 12H. She was raised in a foster home and has had contact with the courts. D. had dropped out of school after the eleventh grade due to pregnancy. For a short time she worked as a cashier in a grocery store. Presently, D. receives assistance from the Department of Social Services. She stated that she would take a job if she could find suitable care for her child.

2.   Female, age nineteen, dropped out of school after completing the eleventh grade. C. became addicted to drugs and completed a nine-month period with the Rockefeller Program for rehabilitation. C. then worked as a telephone operator, but was returned to the program when it was discovered that she was using drugs again. Her visit led to two sessions devoted largely to talk of drug abuse.

3.   Male, age seventeen, dropped out of school in the tenth grade. He had worked in a grocery store. At contact, M. was not working and was using drugs.

4.   Female, age fifteen, was a relative of 5H and 6H. She had a problem in her family life and, as a result, had lived in the homes of friends and other relatives. She was enrolled in school but attended sporadically. S. had frequently been placed in juvenile homes. She had no work experience.

5.   Male, eighteen years old, was the son of a black American mother and a

black Cuban father. He had experienced prejudice because of his race and ethnic identity. Although he had worked for a time as a postal worker, at contact he was not working.

6. Female, age eighteen, mother of one, had dropped out of school in the twelfth grade. She had no previous work experience. She was living with the family of her baby's father.

7. Female, age seventeen, had one child and was expecting another. She had dropped out of school in the ninth grade during her first pregnancy. She had no work experience and received aid from the Department of Social Services.

8. Female, sixteen years old, dropped out of school in the sixth grade. She had no work experience, lived with her father and siblings. Both the mother and stepmother were deceased.

9. Female, age eighteen, was sister of (8) above. She was enrolled in the eleventh grade but did not attend regularly. She held a part-time job in a local grocery store.

10. Female, age nineteen, was a mother of one. Although she had had some work experience, she now received assistance from the Department of Social Services. She was attending Manhattan Community College in the SEEK Program (Search for Education, Elevation and Knowledge).

11. Male, eighteen years old, was the oldest brother of 7H. He had completed the eleventh grade before dropping out of school. He had had several contacts with the police and other agencies. In addition, he had become addicted to narcotics but did not appear to be aware of his sister's, 7H's, involvement with drugs.

12. Female was the fifteen-year-old sister of 7H. She was in the ninth grade until she had to stop attending school due to pregnancy.

13. Mother of 5H and 6H was an attractive and youthful women in her mid-thirties with thirteen children. She emigrated from the South at the age of seventeen where she completed eight years of school. She had experience in factory work. Presently, she is receiving assistance from the Department of Social Services.

14. Female, seventeen years old, (7B) cousin of 10H, whose family moved from Brooklyn to Harlem just before she joined the Job Corps. She was the first member of the Brooklyn group to meet the Harlem girls, whom she described as "young" and "wild."

The Community: Job Referral and Training Agencies

From June through August 1970 the field staff systematically studied the physical and social characteristics of Central Harlem and Bedford-Stuyvesant. They sought to identify the social networks and places where teenagers congregated. Site visits were made to the central and neighborhood-based agencies concerned with teenage training and employment to review their program materials; to confer with key administrators and program personnel; and to observe the actual operation of these agencies. The report on these neighborhood job referral and training agencies presents another aspect of the communities where the study population lives. Tables 5-5 and 5-6 show the agencies visited.

Although a major goal of the project was to contact a target population in the community—their peers and families—an important part of the project was to identify the network of agencies with which these girls do or could come in contact. The field contacts were classified into two general groups: the first category of agencies was the employment/vocational service projects; and the second category was the "other-service" agencies, whose primary concerns are not employment or training—the youth centers, the public and private social service agencies, and the special problem centers such as those for unwed mothers and drug programs. Another aspect of the field activity sought to collect information on companies that would probably employ young women. Though there were no direct staff contacts with the New York City Board of Education, some information was collected on the public school system.

The project staff used a number of different approaches in order to acquire information about the manpower development and employment services in New York City. The staff visited communities and local agencies, interviewed program administrators and government officials, and obtained information from members of the target population. During group sessions, Brooklyn and Harlem resource assistants discussed their personal experiences with some of the agencies. They participated in job hunts for which they were asked to make specific observations about agencies and companies. Resource assistants also revealed some things about their knowledge of the agencies through working on the questionnaires. In addition, friends of group members gave information about their experiences. During field visits, the staff met with members of the target population who were participants in these programs. Finally, staff members read about projects in previous studies and in the publications of the agencies. (See bibliography.)

The staff familiarized itself with the major agencies organized to service the job-seeking and counseling needs of the poverty areas under study. The Economic Development Council of New York City in its study of publicly financed manpower programs in 1970 reported:

> New York City's publicly-financed manpower programs constitute a
> fragmented disjointed, overlapping conglomerate which did not develop
> as the result of an overall, systematic plan, with careful delimitation of
> substantive areas and rational division of responsibility. . . . Demarca-
> tion lines between program responsibilities often do not reflect well-
> planned allocations of functions, but rather the relative power positions,

Table 5-5
Agencies Visited in Harlem by Field Staff
June-September 1970

	Date of Contact	Agency	Type of Program
1.	6/22/70	Manpower & Career Development Agency (MCDA)[a]	Manpower Agency of NYC, Human Resource Administration
2.	7/10/70	Bureau of Labor Statistics (BLS)[a]	New York Regional Office
3.	7/22/70	Assemblyman Southall's Office	Political office; no referrals.
4.	7/22/70	Youth Development Center (YDC)	Cultural and recreational activities.
5.	7/23/70	Mid-Manhattan Adult Training Center	Remedial, vocational prep and occupational skills training—WIN, CEP, MDTA.
6.	7/23/70	HARYOU-NMSC	MCDA community referral and counseling center for all publicly-funded training project jobs.
7.	7/23/70	Urban League	Main office in Harlem, making referrals to Urban League Education Office.
8.	7/23/70	Jones Employment Agency	Private employment agency, serves no one under eighteen years old.
9.	7/23/70	Harlem New York State Employment Center	Referrals and counseling for adults; refers young people to Youth Opportunity Center (YOC).
10.	7/27/70	Job Corps	Screening and counseling office for men's and women's Job Corps.
11.	7/27/70	P.S. 139 Manhattan	Youth Development Center, basic education and recreation.
12.	7/29/70	Neighborhood Youth Corps (NYC)	Located in Harlem, Urban League administered.
13.	7/29/70	Concentrated Employment Program (CEP)	Administration and referral office.
14.	7/29/70	Adolescent Maternity Program	Maternal and Infant Care Program (MIC); services unwed mothers-to-be, age fourteen and over.
15.	7/29/70	MCDA Region 4 Administrative Office	Administrative office.
16.	8/4/70	Harlem Teams for Self-Help	Remedial and continuing education; vocational training, counseling and referrals.

[a]Located outside of target area.

Table 5-5 (continued)

	Date of Contact	Agency	Type of Program
17.	8/4/70	Harlem Prep	Non-Board of Education preparatory school; sends most grads to college with scholarships.
18.	8/4/70	Minisink-New York Mission Society Center	Recreational facilities, mainly for small children.
19.	8/4/70	Kennedy Center	Recreational and remediation mainly for in-school youth.
20.	8/5/70	Youth Services Agency (YSA)	Mainly services for young males.
21.	8/5/70	Milbank-Frawley Model Cities Youth Service Offices	Community planning office; planning multiproblem services.
22.	8/5/70	Urban League Economic Development and Employment	Counseling and referrals; all ages, male and female.
23.	8/5/70	New York State Referral Office	A temporary office to handle questions re: State Office Building.
24.	8/7/70	Youth Opportunity Center (YOC)[a]	New York State Employment Service (NYSES) office for sixteen-twenty-one-year-olds out of school; referrals and counseling for jobs and training.
25.	8/17/70	Upper West Side Community Corporation	Community Corporation for Upper West Side (covers parts of Harlem not covered by HARYOU).
26.	9/15/70	St. Mary's Church-Ackley Community Center	Recreational and study facilities; also NYSES counselor.
27.	9/15/70	Morningside Heights Inc.	Recreation and remediation for Morningside young people, jointly sponsored by civic groups and Columbia University.
28.	9/21/70	Milbank-Frawley Housing Council	Mainly concerned with area housing problems; but makes job referrals to N.Y. Telephone Company, YOC, etc.
29.	9/21/70	Dunlevy-Milbank Center	Recreation, remedial assistance, counseling, some job referral activities.
30.	9/21/70	Afro-American East	Mainly unwed mothers, multiservices.
31.	9/21/70	St. Phillips Community Center	Independent community center – recreational, educational, cultural programs.
32.	9/22/70	Reality House	Drug addicts rehabilitation program.
33.	9/24/70	Upper Manhattan Branch YWCA	Services for young women, currently no employment program.

[a]Located outside of target area.

Table 5-6
Agencies Visited in Bedford-Stuyvesant by Field Staff
June-October 1970

	Date of Contact	Agency	Type of Program
34.	6/9/70	Youth in Action (YIA)	Multiservice umbrella organization. (Community Corporation.)
35.	6/17/70	YIA-NMSC (Neighborhood Manpower Service Center)	Counseling and referrals for jobs/training open to all ages; jointly run by MCDA and YIA.
36.	6/24/70	YIA-NMSC	Outstation of main office.
37.	8/7/70	Project Teen Aid[a]	Public high school in Fort Greene section of Brooklyn for unwed mothers-to-be.
38.	9/23/70	Central Brooklyn Model Cities[a]	Community planning office; handles applicants for civil service positions.
39.	9/29/70	Brooklyn Adult Training Center (BATC)	Training center; remedial, vocational prep, and occupational skills training.
40.	9/29/70	New York State Employment Center	Job training, referrals and counseling for adults—refer youth to YOC.
41.	9/29/70	Young Mothers	YIA—run high school for unwed mothers; education, counseling and job referrals.
42.	10/27/70	Youth Opportunity Center (YOC)[a]	NYSES office servicing sixteen-twenty-one-year-olds, with certificate stating they have left high school; counseling and referrals.
43.	10/27/70	Training Resources for Youth (TRY)	Vocational training for young *males only*.
44.	10/27/70	Stuyvesant Community Center	Health services, recreational facilities and supposedly employment assistance.

[a]Located outside of target area.

at given points in time, of all the competing governmental departments
and agencies anxious to obtain parts of the administrative authority
and portions of the funds allotted for manpower training.[11]

The Economic Development Council has indicated that since 1970 enormous
progress has been made in developing control through the Manpower Area Planning Council and restructuring of the City's Human Resources Administration.

The field staff made trips to Harlem and Bedford-Stuyvesant in search of
centers. They contacted agencies such as community corporations and asked for
guides to the relevant projects. Suggestions from community residents and the
personnel at these agencies were explored. There were several basic questions:

1.   What were the major activities of the particular center?

   a.   Employment problems of the community, or with other needs?
   b.   If an employment agency, what major functions were performed—
        referral, counseling, training?
   c.   Where were job-seekers referred?

2.   Were services provided for members of the target population? Do
members of the target population visit these agencies?

3.   What agencies existed in the community that served manpower or
employment needs of the community? What were the sponsoring/funding
agencies and what networks existed between agencies?

4.   What impressions did the project staff gain from agency staff concerning services and problems, particularly as they affect the efforts of members
of our target population to find training and jobs?

The field staff did an extensive, although by no means comprehensive,
survey of the community agencies and major training job and referral programs.
Contact was made with over forty agencies. For some agencies the staff was
able to pair staff-gathered information with information related by resource
assistants.

Some general statements that can be made regarding the field work impressions of the agencies were:

1.   Many referral and training centers were not known to the community.
The offices were not clearly "marqueed"; their functions were disguised. In
general, agencies did not publicize their location or services. Outreach to the
community was in many cases nonexistent.

2.   Among the employment/training agencies, the needs of teenage girls
were given low priority. Many programs did not accept people under eighteen;
many of the programs designed for those under eighteen were in "male trades"
and did not accept females. Also, some counselors did not refer young girls to
the programs that were open to them.

3.   Employment needs were given low priority in many of the programs
in which young black girls were participating, such as remedial education,
cultural and personal care orientation, and recreation.

4.   Efficient organization and coordination of the employment resources in the city appeared to be more of a goal than reality. The communications channels that supposedly exist, facilitated by mechanisms, such as the computerized job banks, did not function fully because of budget problems, administrative conflicts, and inadequate knowledge of job and training opportunities.

The staff learned that the girls under study were ineligible for many of the training programs. Employer hiring preference works against the young, unskilled, and inexperienced work-seekers. The young, dropout, unwed mother is seen as an employment risk. Given the current economic situation, openings for regular employment and company/government-sponsored training programs were few, and screening processes had become more rigid. However, it was noted that the centers were severely understaffed for the client loads they had. In addition, their outreach was very limited.

There were many impressions gained that created a more total view of services. Rules and policies that seemed straightforward enough when explained, took on new meaning when placed in context. For example, the requirement of certain documents seemed reasonable. However, obtaining them entailed one long waiting line after another and travel to different parts of the city with no guarantee of a job.

Reputation and image were important in the communications network with poverty neighborhoods—especially within a particular peer group. Girls seeking alternatives to their out-of-work, out-of-school state asked friends about opportunities. Girls passed on this information about the business establishments and organizations.

Frequently the information was distorted. Whether the information was based on personal experiences or hearsay was unknown and unimportant to the receiver of the information—she acted according to what she had heard. If she was told that jobs were available and she had the qualifications, she might apply; if she was told that a certain organization had no programs that suited her needs, or that the organization had a reputation for building up hopes that were never satisfied, or that paychecks were never distributed on time, she was likely not to visit that particular agency or apply for that program. Many girls believed that if a situation did not suit friends it would not suit them.

Schools

The institution with which all of our resource assistants, and presumably most girls in the target population, have had contact is the New York City Public School System. The experiences in school may be a determinant of current school/employment status, attitudes toward work and future occupations of these young women.

Most of the Harlem resource assistants were frustrated by a school system

that did not allow them to take the courses they wanted and did not provide
them with the information desired and needed about jobs and higher education.
The girls cited instances in which they felt teachers and guidance counselors
had passed on incomplete or incorrect information and had practiced racial
discrimination; they felt that red tape and the absence of appeals channels made
change impossible. These attitudes were common among girls in Brooklyn and
in Manhattan, whether they were in school or out of school during the project.

In a detailed study of entry into the labor market, Sally Hillsman Baker
has documented how racial differences in economic achievement of graduates
from one vocational high school in New York City were directly related to how
the school functioned as a gatekeeper to the labor market and a selector of
talent. "—the school is the locus of a stratification system. In selecting among
eligibles the stratification system operates so that individuals from groups
already ranked differently in the society at large come to occupy places in the
school's ranking system consistent with the societal status structure."[12] The
experiences of the minority students in the school's internal stratification system
affected their motivation to succeed and their aspirations.

Baker was able to track the income of these graduates over a seven-and-
a-half-year period and found that whites averaged higher earnings than the
minority graduates. Even where education and training were identical (placement into and graduation from the elite curriculum track), the minority graduates were less able than whites to translate these into similar levels of income.

The study group was asked to respond to questions on what school had
meant to them. Their responses reflect the differences among them in attitude,
ability to understand the questions and express ideas, and their moods at the
time the questions were asked.

Question: What has school meant to you?
              (A) What years/people/events are outstanding in your mind and
              why?
              (B) What has caused you the most trouble?

2H (enrolled in school): "School has meant meeting and having many wonder-
              ful friends. It also means an education to me."
              (A) "All my years in school have been both rewarding and
              memorable."
              (B) "Parents have caused me the most trouble."

3H (high school graduate): "In elementary school, I went because I had to. In
              junior high school, I can't remember much about it."
              (A) "In high school becoming the G.O. Vice President. I learned
              a lot. I believe I became a much better person, socially and
              intellectually."

      (B) "I had just one problem with a teacher in school."

4H (dropout): "Everything."
      (A) "High school and basketball."
      (B) "Family."

5H (dropout): "Nothing, don't like teachers; like two subjects, math and home economics."

6H (dropout): "Nothing."
      (A) "First grade I like the teachers."
      (B) "School and staying out late."

7H (dropout):
      (A) "Place to go to keep kids off the street and at the same time, get a little bit of knowledge for your elderly life, good jobs, etc."
      (B) "Playing hookie; having a good time."

8H (enrolled in school): "It meant a whole lot to me because nowadays you can't get a good job without an education."
      (A) "All years some people were nice and some weren't. Well, we really don't have too many events that happen but one, and that is the talent show."

9H (enrolled in school): "Eighth year, we all moved close to each other, honor roll, and graduation. Some of the work was kind of hard."

11H (enrolled in school): "It meant I could make a living without going through changes."

12H (dropout): "Nothing important or exciting."
      (B) "Not too much trouble; dropout."

6B (dropout): "To me school is O.K., but you can't trust the teachers."

Many of the girls believed that the education system forced them to follow an unsatisfactory prescribed curriculum. Several of the resource assistants who became interested in a particular area of study, such as mathematics, felt that they were not allowed to explore that area. Many of the girls in the academic and general tracks stated that counselors would not schedule them for commercial courses that could better prepare them for the work world. The girls also expressed the view that programs to prepare them for jobs were inaccessible.

Girls who had been enrolled in special high schools or training programs, such as the unwed mothers' programs, commented that they were pleased with the apparent practicality of their courses, as well as the more relaxed atmosphere that was more conducive to learning.

While school authorities, community groups, and some parents stress the value of a high school diploma, many young black girls are not convinced that this is essential to, or a guarantee of, success in the world of work. Many girls seemed to believe that a high school equivalency diploma is not as good as a regular high school diploma. At the same time, girls knew from their own experience and from their friends' tales that experience and particular job skills are sometimes more important than the actual diploma. One young woman who said she had done well in school decided during her senior year that it would be to her advantage to enter an adult training center and develop good secretarial skills instead of remaining in the public high school to which she spent a great deal of time traveling in an unsafe neighborhood and where drug and racial problems among other students interfered with her education.

The fact that New York State high schools offer three diplomas—academic, general, and commercial—is a source of some difficulty for many young people. Many who feel capable of completing a college preparatory program believe that teachers do not encourage enrollment in the academic course, and so they choose the general curriculum. Others, who want to go on for higher education but feel they will have to work at least part-time, are discouraged by the difficulty of acquiring commercial skills while they are academic students.

A report released by the Community Service Society of New York noted that students on the lowest academic level were transferred to the general course in academic high schools. It concluded that "the 'dumping ground' for the academically retarded has shifted in large measure from the vocational schools to the general course in the academic schools."[13]

The schools are a constant source of trouble and frustration for youth and their parents in Harlem and Bedford-Stuyvesant, where racial (black against Puerto Rican when not black against white) and teacher disputes are frequent and marijuana and drugs are readily available. Girls expressed dismay at the police-state atmosphere in many of their schools.

The high rate of school dropout among urban ghetto youths is often cited as a major factor when discussing the prevalence of crime and unemployment. It is difficult to arrive at an accurate figure showing dropouts from school, but figures can be obtained on the numbers of employment certificates issued, the "over seventeen" who leave school, and the enrollees who do not attend school and are not found.

That a young person is enrolled in school is not an indicator that he is being satisfactorily educated, or even that he attends school. The average daily attendance (ADA) figure in the public academic high schools has been falling, annually, although enrollment has increased. ADA was below 70 percent in Brooklyn and below 65 percent in Manhattan. In both boroughs, the ADA was significantly lower in the schools with the lowest percentages of white enrollees. The girls talked freely about the difference between being "enrolled in school" and actually attending classes regularly and attentively.

An indicator of the academic performance of youth attending poverty area schools is the reading level recorded in junior high schools. The average reading scores in *all* the junior high schools within the Bedford-Stuyvesant and Harlem communities are below grade level. The students who complete junior high school in these areas are likely to enter high school with severe reading deficiencies, which affect overall academic performance, create some social pressure, and may contribute to the decision of many to leave school.

While reading problems are prevalent, many girls do not read because they are not interested in the material. It is of some interest that all of the girls in the Harlem group, regardless of grade level attained or level of reading, read and discussed the book *Coming of Age in Mississippi*, included as a special activity.

Statistics on the unemployment of high school graduates and dropouts for 1971 reveal significant differences between the two groups for all teenage females. For black young women between sixteen and twenty-one, the rates are 19.2 percent and 28.2 percent, respectively.

Unemployment Rates, 1969[14]

	Percent
16-17 years old	
Graduate*	15.5
Dropout	34.4
18-19 years old	
Graduate*	9.1
Dropout	20.8

*Out-of-school high school graduate.

As we shall see later, the high school diploma is the first requirement from the employer for consideration as a "permanent" employee in the New York City labor market.

Drugs

Despite the prevalence of drug abuse and the easy availability of drugs in the New York area, teenage females in our study population showed wide variation in their knowledge of, attitudes toward, and personal experience with drugs. A recent study noted that 6 percent of the population in the Central Harlem Health District is addicted.[15]

The Brooklyn group had very little knowledge of drugs, unanimously voiced disapproval of drug use, and denied experimentation or experience with any type of drug. The complete avoidance behavior of the teenage females in the Brooklyn group may be partly associated with their rural, close family, and in-group orientations.

In contrast, the members of the Harlem group had extensive knowledge of drugs as well as of pushers and buyers. Knowledge about drugs and firsthand experience with drug use and drug users seemed to help many of them to weigh the consequences of drug use more realistically. They recognized the need for strong individual motivation to avoid becoming "hooked" and to break the habit. They reported on the easy availability of drugs. The group shared negative feelings about hard drugs but had few reservations about "pot." They freely discussed their parents' concern about drugs—one family bribed the resource assistant with the promise to buy her anything she wanted if she stayed off drugs. They recognized that boys in the community were more heavily involved than were girls, and they indicated that they were concerned about their relationships with boys who used drugs.

Black Awareness and Racial Attitudes

When the Harlem resource assistants were recruited, they were told that their help was needed in conducting a project to better the employment opportunities for young black girls. To some this meant that they would attempt to "crack discrimination," and this thought generated a certain amount of enthusiasm. Some of the girls in the group, however, might not have felt that they needed to reflect on "blackness"—they live out the consequences of being poor and black every day.

We attempted to ascertain their degree of awareness of current activities to strengthen black pride and to build political and economic power. Some girls used the term *colored*, others said *black*, and a few used these terms— along with Negro and Afro-American—interchangeably. On two occasions the girls increased their knowledge and enjoyment of black culture: a visit to the Schomburg Collection and a performance by a theatre group, the "Black Experience."

The girls were asked to write briefly on what it means to be black in America. Predictably the attitudes varied. The answers also reflected their willingness and ability to express themselves.

Question: What does it mean to you to be black in America?

1H:	"I have been living here so long that it doesn't mean anything."
2H:	"Being black means having a sense of pride and ambition. A strong desire to continually better myself and my financial status. My wish is to make this white society realize that I'm *somebody*."
3H:	"I have so much pride in being black, that my head is in the sky and I can't see because the clouds are in the way."
4H:	"Someone who has to show the white man that I am also a person, I am also human. I'm just somebody."
5H:	"Nothing—it means to be poor, but it means to be a part of America only."
6H:	"I don't think it makes any difference in the colors."
7H:	"I'm proud to be black. I have all the opportunities I could want. I just hope in time I take them before its too late."
8H:	"It means to me to still be in a worser position than the blacks who were slaves long ago. Because they are killing everybody who tries to help the blacks, or is black."
9H:	"To be proud. Long time ago people called us colored. What I wanted to know, what is a *colored* person?"
10H:	"Nothing really because to me it's not the color, it is the person."
11H:	"It means to me that you have to go through so many changes with your own phoney people and the system. Only some make it without being brainwashed. Once a blackie gets there he knows no one else. If a black person helps just one person, it would be all right in black America."
12H:	"To be black in America is to be proud of what you really are, black!!"
3B:	"Well, if you are a girl or a boy, sometimes you cannot get a good job. Because you don't have the schooling for it and sometimes you can't live where you want to live."
6B:	"It means a lot to me because I am proud of my race."

On several occasions, there were discussions about race attitudes. The study group discussed the problems that exist between blacks and Puerto Ricans and black and whites in the schools. Difficulties with teachers were identified as racial as well as functions of the generation gap. Most of the group members felt that their contacts with and observations of white youth were sufficient enough to make them hopeful about the future of race relations.

Conflicts within the black community in America were mentioned. Many heated arguments developed, and frequent subtle allusions were made regarding the relationship of the black bourgeoisie to the less well educated, lower-income, ghetto blacks. Criticisms included the assumptions that few black doctors and lawyers really understand the feelings and problems of their ghetto clients, that the children of these professionals and other middle-class people do not grow up really knowing what it means to be black because they do not live in or visit the ghetto; and that because of their inability to understand and relate, they are thus not able to help. One articulate, well-read, young woman sharply criticized those who leave the ghetto as soon as they can afford to; but she later stated that she hoped she would be able to finish college, marry, and raise children who would have an easier childhood than she. She admitted that she would prefer to do this in an environment with better housing and less crime.

Some discussions involved the exploitation of blacks by blacks—how pimps and other gangsters make money off the people, abuse women and children, and keep their own families protected from the evils of the streets. The girls also discussed receiving especially "hard" treatment from black teachers and black supervisors. They felt that some blacks, once they assumed responsible positions, forgot that they were black, and did not help their "brothers."

Black awareness was related to employment problems mainly through heated discussions about whether blacks should accept some jobs purely for the sake of having a job. Some felt strongly that domestic work should not be accepted; others recognized that in earlier years this was the only kind of work available. It was believed that no girls today should accept such positions, but rather that "better" positions must be demanded. Another opinion was that it was OK to be a cleaning woman in an office building or hotel, but that maid's work in a private white household should not be considered.

The study group may be keenly aware of the significant changes in the employment of black women as domestic servants. The 1970 census data reveal a sizable occupational shift into jobs in health services, cleaning services, and food services sectors. Almost three-fourths of the black women who remain in this occupation reside in the South and are over forty-five years of age.[16] Thus, these young women know adult black women who work as hospital attendants, community aides, or food-service helpers for large employers. There is little reason to believe that they should perceive employment in household service to be rewarding.

Both the Harlem and Brooklyn group members were aware of discrimination against blacks in the world of work. Several girls had experienced hostility and prejudice on job hunts and recognized the lower status adult black workers held in companies in which they had worked or with which they interviewed. One researcher has noted that low incomes and inadequate employment opportunities for blacks and other minorities were among the most important human resource development problems of the 1960s and are likely to remain so, although hopefully with diminishing intensity. In addition he stated,

> It became increasingly clear that institutionalized racial patterns were more deeply rooted and pervasive than the more overt forms of discrimination. . . . Institutionalized racial practices affected all aspects of life—education, housing, jobs, social affairs—and caused

the persons discriminated against not to aspire to or prepare for the kinds of jobs from which they had been barred.[17]

The resource assistants also took note during their job hunts that few officials and managers were members of minority groups. They realized in their contacts with personnel and supervisory workers—those positions concerned with hiring, firing, promotion, and decision making—that few blacks held such positions. Black workers may have their mobility options severely restricted because they are perceived in the labor market as less productive and achievement-oriented than majority workers. Differential treatment in the labor market has undermined the occupational standing and economic status of blacks.

Employment discrimination as measured by the ratio of expected lifetime earnings of whites with a given level of school to the expected lifetime earnings of blacks with a similar level of schooling shows that blacks benefit less than whites in terms of increased income. . . . The detailed 1970 census data should throw more light on the ambiguous role of education for blacks as reflected in their enormous difficulties in labor markets.[18]

Conclusions

This chapter presented detailed information on the girls and their communities. The most significant findings were:

1. The adults, parents and guardians of young black females in New York City poverty areas have not fared well in the labor market. Because they have experienced much unemployment and underemployment and have generally held low-wage jobs, they cannot present enviable images of working adults to the youths of the area.

2. Black families who are below the proverty level in urban ghettos are not a homogeneous group despite similarities of their surface characteristics. Varied patterns of family structure exist.

3. The seven home visits with families of the Harlem group members revealed that parents' stated expectations for their children's future only partially influence the youth. Young people also gain impressions of the economic struggle and labor force participation by observing their parents' difficulties and achievements.

4. The staff surveyed referral and training agencies in Central Harlem and Bedford-Stuyvesant and discovered that young female teenagers were not involved in most of the manpower programs.

5. The girls were often frustrated by the school system. They felt that teachers and guidance counselors had passed on incomplete or incorrect information regarding jobs and higher education. Prejudicial attitudes among school staffs was believed to be present.

6.   Prevalence of drug abuse and easy availability exist in the New York area. Brooklyn group members were poorly informed about drugs, voiced disapproval of drug abuse, and denied experimentation with any kind of drugs. On the other hand, Harlem group girls were quite knowledgeable of drug use, pushers, and buyers. They recognized that boys in the community were more heavily involved with drugs than girls.

7.   Like black people all over the United States, the resource assistants voiced varied opinions concerning black awareness and racial attitudes.

A more detailed discussion of the employment/training and community agencies appears in the appendix to this chapter.

Appendix 5A: Survey of Job Referral and Training

The staff started to examine the employment centers by visiting offices linked to the New York City Manpower and Career Development Agency (MCDA) and the New York State Employment Service (NYSES). The New York State Employment Service maintains offices in poverty neighborhoods as well as in downtown areas. Youth Opportunity Centers (YOC) were established to assist the out-of-school young person by providing counseling and referring him/her to jobs or training. Also, New York State Employment Service counselors had offices in public schools, in some training centers, and in some independent youth centers. Thus, if the young person was aware of these resources, there would be ample opportunity to contact counselors.

The staff talked with a YOC administrator in Brooklyn who said that services were provided for out-of-school youth who had statements indicating that they were not planning to return to school. Thus, nongraduates have been asked to go back to the schools which they last attended—a trip some youth would not want to make. Young people in search of jobs were not always given proper information or directions.

A resource assistant in Brooklyn told of her visit to one of the NYSES centers for adults. Although the receptionist knew that she was only seventeen, she was told to wait. Later she was sent to another center, but never met with a counselor. She was not referred to the YOC or a school counselor. NYSES youth counselors themselves spoke of a bleak picture for placing young females. The demands for jobs far exceeded the positions employers were offering young, inexperienced females. Because of lack of work experience, high school graduates often were not in a better competitive position than school dropouts.

In New York City, counseling and referral were handled by the Manpower and Career Development Agency (MCDA). Training and remedial education programs were administered and slots filled through MCDA. The agency maintained a computerized system for matching job-seekers and prospective employers. Community residents contacted the MCDA services through Neighborhood Manpower Service Centers (NMSC) and Regional Opportunity Centers located in the eleven manpower regions. Job and skills seekers could also be referred to programs under MCDA contracts.

MCDA has placed emphasis on employing *males* and people categorized in the following order of priorities within the "universe of needs":

1. welfare recipients (especially welfare mothers)

2. school dropouts
3. underemployed minority group members
4. the handicapped
5. undereducated and chronically unemployed.

Many black teenage girls were welfare recipients, school dropouts, under-educated, and living in environments that destined them for chronic unemployment. The staff did not succeed in obtaining statistics about the actual servicing of the target population by MCDA.

The MCDA Regional Manpower System and computer service was supposed to provide well coordinated, easily accessible answers to the manpower needs of those New York City residents who use public job/training-seeking channels. There was limited evidence of coordination and free flow of current information among the branches of this system. The staff made contact with the MCDA system at different levels and through different procedures.

While conducting the early neighborhood tours in Bedford-Stuyvesant, the field staff members located the Neighborhood Manpower Service Center operated by Youth In Action, the area's community corporation. The staff entered the reception area used by all clients and visitors, and they were requested to sign in. Arrangements were made to permit the staff to meet with the center director. While the staff waited, it was noted that most of the clients were adults. This first meeting with a program official was a learning experience for field staff in terms of: gaining a view of channels in a center; understanding the necessary tact that must be used in approaching center staff; and learning to develop questions that would yield the information needed, and promote discussion and interest in the project while not taking much staff time during unscheduled visits.

Three casually, but neatly dressed, young black staff members entered the office of the director and identified themselves as members of an action research project concerned about unemployment among black teenage girls. The staff was received rather suspiciously. The project director introduced his assistant, a black woman who was perhaps in her thirties. Inquiries concerning the extent to which follow-up of clients was stressed and performed by NMSC staff caused the project director to become increasingly defensive and curt. Although the assistant provided the staff with a great deal of information about NMSC and the MCDA and suggested means of getting more information, her manner was hurried. This was interpreted as hostility and self-protection. The staff visit was interpreted as an evaluation of the center's performance. We later realized that both staff members were sensitive because their program did not run efficiently and the demands on the center were too great—more people than could be serviced properly were appearing. Follow-up was impossible, unless the doors were to be closed to new clients. There was insufficient staff to compile and analyze the statistics on the clientele; the computer, one of the innovations most highly prized by the MCDA, was not in service because of a variety of financial difficulties between the community corporation and MCDA; and there was inadequate space for counselors and training classes to operate. The assistant director discussed the intake procedure, the relationship of YIA-NMSC to the MCDA Regional Manpower System, and the fact that Bedford-Stuyvesant is the only poverty area in New York which is not wholly within a single Manpower Region.

This group had contact with a counselor at a YIA-NMSC outstation located in another section within the Bedford-Stuyvesant area. Here the counselor, a young Puerto Rican woman, was most interested in the project and was quite willing to divulge information about her ability to service clients, her conflicts with her supervisors at the central NMSC, her frequent ignoring of boundaries in order to serve people who lived outside of her service area, and the paper work that took up so much of her time.

The staff also had contact with the HARYOU-NMSC in Harlem. The staff was apprehensive about making contact with this and other organizations in Harlem because of the association of MARC's president with HARYOU, and his role in the black community. Yet this kind of political problem was not encountered. The staff was unable to obtain much information from the person in charge of this dark, secluded center. Whether this was because it was midsummer, late in the day, and the visit was unscheduled is still undetermined. Nevertheless, the center did not appear to be equipped to handle many clients at one time, and it is likely that a person walking down 145th Street, hoping to find an employment center without a specific address, would never have spotted this employment referral/counseling center. The center was located above a local assemblyman's office and was not clearly identifiable.

An overview of a first visit to a Neighborhood Manpower Service Center is: first, one must see an intake clerk, fill out forms, speak with a counselor, and hope that the counselor has information about some opening for training or jobs that in some way match the skills and job requirements of the client. The openings were generally in low-paying jobs, jobs that were undesirable to the client, and jobs with experience or skill requirements not possessed by the client. Many of the training programs listed by MCDA for referral were in "male" trades; others were open only to welfare recipients or those living in certain neighborhoods.

A special problem existed in Brooklyn, where residents of two or three Manpower Regions were serviced by the same NMSC. One person would be assigned a place in a new class in his area's Regional Opportunity Center, but a neighbor or friend living close by seeking to be placed in the same class would find that he was serviced by another Regional Opportunity Center.

The target population possessed limited knowledge about these services. Discussions with resource assistants in Harlem and Brooklyn revealed that none knew of the existence or location of the NMSCs; a few were aware of the community corporations.

During several trips to NMSCs we noted that young females did not appear to be the clientele. We discounted these centers as sources of contact for the study group. The NMSC staff insisted that girls occasionally came in, but were unable to give the percentages of females nor help us contact girls.

One of the resource assistants visited the Brooklyn central NMSC, waited three hours, was interviewed, and told that nothing was available but that she would be called if something came up. Center personnel said that they were aware that no outreach or recruitment was done in the community. However, they insisted that they could not service more clients. As a result, they did not encourage further publicity.

Knowledge of what centers or companies offered, whether factual or "grapevine misinformation," was important in determining where girls would go, if they decided to seek jobs or training. When the resource assistants discussed employment or vocational training they either referred friends to or dissuaded friends from certain programs. The staff visited the Job Corps office in the Theresa Towers, centrally located in the Harlem business district. A young black male screener and counselor discussed problems of the residential women's Job Corps program, noting that lesbianism was a major problem. A member of the Harlem group had mentioned that the prevalence of lesbianism had contributed to her decision to leave her training site within a week. On the other hand, a Brooklyn group member sent home a favorable report of her Job Corps experience in New Mexico, and her cousin, a Harlem resource assistant who had become increasingly dissatisfied with her high school program and home situation, has mentioned that she is interested in the Job Corps program.

Harlem Teams for Self-Help was apparently a very popular program. It was known by young people in Brooklyn and throughout Harlem. One resource assistant participated in the program during the fall and winter of 1970 and had generally favorable comments. The program is located in very old, drab facilities, but the administrators seemed to be pleased with their reputation. They had a remedial education program and prevocational training as well as some occupational skills training. In addition, Harlem Teams maintained an independent employment service. This service did not provide many jobs for girls of the target population. The impression of the staff was that the Harlem Teams was not equipped to give much guidance to young women who had limited knowledge of work and unrealistic or nonexistent career plans.

One of our resource assistants completed the Harlem Teams program and was then placed at the New York Adult Training Center in lower Manhattan. Another Harlem resource assistant was interested in the Harlem Teams program. She was told by her Job Corps counselor that she should have given her age as seventeen (even though she was only sixteen) because the program maintains an inflexible enforcement of its minimum-age requirement. Harlem Teams is one of the very few programs run specifically for the training needs of young poverty neighborhood residents.

Another program, the Neighborhood Youth Corps (NYC), has been severely criticized because of unrealistic work situations and poor administration. Nevertheless, it provides income for teenagers during the winter after school and during the summer. The staff visited the administration offices in Bedford-Stuyvesant. No information was obtained; the small office was occupied only by some young people. In Harlem, the staff met with the Harlem NYC project director at the Urban League office. On that afternoon, he was being sought after by young people who wanted their checks. Check distribution has always been a major problem for NYC programs in New York.

The staff made two visits to two vocational centers (Mid-Manhattan Adult Training Center and the Brooklyn Adult Training Center) where students were enrolled in MDTA, CEP, WIN, and other publicly funded programs. Both centers operated in dilapidated public school buildings where the old drab furniture and noisy signal system remained. Reception of the staff at both centers was pleasant; however, one fact became evident early in our contacts: few of the students were members of the sixteen-to-nineteen-year-old black female population with which we wanted to make contact.

One of the early questions of the project concerning field exploration was whether agencies were visible and accessible. As previously stated, many agencies were located above unrelated offices or had signs that did not clearly indicate the exact location and business hours of the office. The staff found that most agencies concerned with the employment needs of Harlem and Bedford-Stuyvesant residents had offices in the poverty neighborhoods. The Harlem community agencies were located in storefronts in different sections of the community. Some programs, such as Job Corps, CEP, and MIC, had offices in the centrally located Theresa Towers.

In Bedford-Stuyvesant, most community agencies were located along a central street near a major business section in the area. Although this area was easily accessible from most parts of Bedford-Stuyvesant by public transportation, there were some agency outstations at other points in the sprawling area.

In Brooklyn, the office of Central Brooklyn Model Cities (CBMC) was a notable exception to the pattern of locating community offices in easily accessible areas. The CBMC headquarters are located in an out-of-the-way dilapidated warehouse area. The staff found that while CBMC did not have regular programs for employment, those who came in would either be screened at the center or referred elsewhere. Many people went to the CBMC to apply for civil service jobs and trainee programs.

Following are some ideas and problems discussed with agency personnel:

1. Many of the agency staff members indicated that they were severely understaffed and unable to provide the kinds of services required by the

centers' rules. Thus, careful investigation of a client's history and employment and training goals, and thorough follow-up on referrals were not done.

2.   Many agency staff members indicated awareness and concern about the needs of the target population. But the agency had not been able to give special attention to this group. In some centers, programs for young women were said to be in the plans for next year. Many said that because they were so understaffed and had difficulty placing members of this age group, they discouraged publicity of services among the group.

3.   Some agency staff members challenged a study project to open employment opportunities for young black women. Not only are government studies viewed with suspicion, but the feeling is strong that it is more important to press for the education and employment of black males.

Special Services and Miscellaneous
Community Offices

In addition to contacting employment and training centers, the staff visited other programs that were addressed primarily to other needs of the target population. Some sixteen-to-nineteen-year-old females had to learn to cope with such problems as drug addiction and pregnancy. These situations interrupted regular schooling and affected availability for employment, while increasing the financial needs of the young girls. The staff had contact with only one drug rehabilitation program, where plans were being made for a program for unwed mothers. Funding is a particularly difficult problem for these programs. The staff spoke with some young women in a black East Harlem organization, Afro-American East, and learned that while it provided job referral and case work services for girls throughout East and Central Harlem, the scope of the services was limited. In most programs for unwed mothers, the emphasis was placed on encouraging the completion of the young mother's education. At the Maternity and Infant Care (MIC) in Harlem, where hospital and school referrals were the primary concern, there was a staff member in charge of vocational counseling. She encouraged the young women to return to school, referred them to HARYOU or Manpower Administration contract company programs, and extended limited help to the young fathers in finding employment.

During the staff's first contacts with high schools for young unwed mothers-to-be, staff members felt that they were being chastised for their concern with girls who were out of school. These programs stressed that a young mother should not interrupt her education to get a job just because she has had a baby.

One of the Brooklyn resource assistants had completed a semester at the nonaccredited Young Mothers School, run by Youth In Action (YIA). She indicated that she had enjoyed the classes and atmosphere more than her regular school. She seemed determined to complete her high school education and begin further vocational training. She also wanted a part-time job. For many determined young women, going to school and working are certainly not mutually exclusive activities.

The high schools for young mothers might have been reluctant to give out information about jobs to girls who have not graduated, but they did attempt to offer the girls the courses they wanted, particularly vocational courses. Public high schools were frequently criticized by the resource assistants for not doing this. The unwed mothers' schools offer courses in commercial skills, home economics, health, and regular academic subjects.

The independent service organizations, such as the Children's Aid Society, the Ys, and the Urban League, were investigated as soon as their centers were called to our attention. Many reported that they would consider employment activities in the future. The staff had no contact with the YWCA staff in Bedford-Stuyvesant, but did visit the YMCA in that area, where many projects for males only were run. A bias against females in many projects affected those girls who had expressed interest in electronics and mechanical work. Training programs in these areas were generally open only to young men.

The Children's Aid Society's Dunlevy-Milbank Center maintained a recreational and remediation program that concentrated on in-school youth rather than dropouts. Yet in the program year 1969–70, they did attempt to become involved with the problems of dropouts by setting up information programs with banks who were hiring young unskilled people without diplomas. The center also made job referrals when requested to do so, usually to the banks and telephone company. The director of the center had reservations about the Neighborhood Youth Corps placements, but stressed the importance of the project as an income source for youth. This center works with the age group comparable to our study group. Outreach activities were limited, however, and staff could not judge how many out-of-work/out-of-school girls had contact with this center. The center director attempted to bring together a group of girls eligible to participate in the Manpower survey but was unable to do so. The staff met with one girl who was "doing nothing." She apparently was not interested in changing her situation by either going to work or back to school.

The staff found that the Urban League was active in Harlem as a referral and counseling organization. During the summer of 1970, a young black man directed the Neighborhood Youth Corps and a number of recreation programs from the Urban League Education Office on 130th Street. This person was willing to take time from a busy schedule to answer questions from the Manpower staff, but did not follow up by obtaining names and statistics regarding the involvement of target population members. The League also maintained an Economic Development and Employment Office on 7th Avenue near 133rd Street. People walked in and requested counseling and job referrals, much the same as at the Neighborhood Manpower Service Centers (NMSC). This center was considerably more visible than the HARYOU-NMSC. The staff was racially integrated. The young white counselor impressed us with her concern for her clients and her knowledge about the job market. Her comments also reminded us of visits to the Brooklyn NMSC offices: more men than women and girls visited the center; there had been difficulty in placing girls on jobs and even more difficulty in placing them on jobs from which satisfaction and long service were expected; there was little point in further publicity of the Economic Development and Employment Office because it was already understaffed for the services it provided.

The staff had assumed that, if nowhere else, out-of-school/out-of-work girls could be found at the community centers. Therefore, the staff visited some centers in Central Harlem and others in the area designated as Morningside Heights. The staff at the Ackley Center, sponsored by St. Mary's Church, was most helpful. This center provided not only study and recreation facilities for in-school youth, but also a New York State Employment Service counselor who could interview, counsel, and make referrals to jobs. The staff's discussion with this counselor revealed that more males than females applied and that placement of males is less difficult than placement of females. This NYSES person was obviously in need of new job slots, and he misinterpreted the Manpower project as a new source of clerical job openings. He gave referral cards to several young females; two came for interviews the next day.

The other centers do some job/training referral. However, emphasis was on keeping the young women in school and involved with constructive after-school activities. We talked with a group of fourteen-to-sixteen-year-olds who participated in regularly scheduled, supervised evening club meetings. These girls were all in school and some were working on career plans; few had work experiences. Those who had searched for jobs knew the frustrations of following ads that were not intended for them.

The staff did not contact any of the night centers in schools or housing projects, but it is known that some of the resource assistants in Harlem participated in them. No one ever mentioned these as sources of employment information.

One area where community agencies could serve as encouraging examples to the girls would have been in providing employment in the center. Discussions with personnel at YIA and help wanted ads for Harlem agencies revealed that these agencies maintain high employment standards. Thus, most of the girls, though eager to be hired and trained, were presently unskilled and inexperienced, and those who might seek clerical positions with these centers would not find them to be eager employers. The staff learned that at one time YIA had a program for hiring and training unskilled clerical and secretarial help, but terminated it because it was considered excessively expensive. One of the Brooklyn resource assistants had gotten her job at YIA when a counselor in a youth group in which she was participating learned that she had clerical skills.

Efforts were being made to give young people work experience in the recreation program as instructors and supervisors at Morningside Heights, Inc., an organization whose sponsors include Columbia University. This program was set up so that job descriptions, a modified promotional ladder, and a wage scale gave the participants goals and a sense of accomplishment. Dunlevy-Milbank, in its day care center, attempted to offer a similar opportunity for earning income, work experience, learning responsibility, and making a contribution to the community.

The staff noticed during community tours of Bedford-Stuyvesant and Harlem many storefront programs with names such as "Self-Help Project." Some Afro stores also have political posters and signs that urge education, training, and economic stability as essentials for the betterment of black people. The suggested focus of many of these places was on adults and males. In many cases, however, the organizations were closed when staff members were in the field and the true nature of these programs was never learned.

Conclusion

The majority of the employment training organizations visited proved to have small, poorly informed staffs. Many of the girls who attempted to utilize such agencies either were asked to wait long periods of time or to complete time-consuming tasks only to find later that they were not in the population that the agency served. The majority of programs run by employment/training organizations did not give priority to the employment and training problems of young females.

Knowledge gained by the girls concerning the agencies and their programs was from the grapevine. Most of this information was distorted. Moreover, many agencies proved to provide inadequate services due to their own financial difficulties and the politics of poverty programs. There was little coordination and referral services among agencies. The miscellaneous community agencies were not employment or training oriented.

6

Employment Problems of Black Teenage Females

A Psychological Perspective on Unemployment

Socialization to work of teenage females from low-income black families should be examined within the context of motivational problems of these poverty populations. What are the positive inner forces that propel an individual to achieve? How can these forces be nurtured or strengthened? How can negative forces that militate against achievement be obliterated, or at least neutralized? A recent study examines two differing views of motivational issues of poverty populations.[1]

The first approach contends that the motivational problems of the poor may stem from the absence of the means necessary for success in the world of work, i.e., the basic disposition, the values, the aspirations, and the beliefs of middle-class society. Hence, the poor must be retaught and resocialized if they are to make an adequate occupational adjustment.

A second approach highlights the motivational problems of powerlessness, the inability to implement aspirations and to attain desired ends. The problem of the poor is not one of different hopes, but of unfulfilled hopes; for them the route between means and ends has been short-circuited. Thus, programs should concentrate on removing the resultant obstacles, whether they reside within the individual (skills) or within society (discrimination).

One way to minimize feelings of powerlessness is to guarantee a real payoff, a job worth holding at the end of training; and the best guarantee of a meaningful job is on-the-job training, supplemented, if necessary, with resocialization-type services (e.g., counseling). Motivational problems of efficacy and expectancy may be as resistant to change as problems of value socialization.

Another motivational issue is oriented to whether control of one's life is vested in external or internal sources, whether one believes oneself guided, for the most part, by internal environment-values, or forces outside the individual like "getting the breaks." Programs generated from an "internal" perspective focus on self-improvement and appeal to individual pride, while proponents of the "external" pole attempt to promote group pride and focus on problems in the environment.

Most literature on this subject supports the position that internal control is a positive motivating force and makes for better adjustment. For job-training programs, the implication is clear; convert the external-control believers into

69

internal-control believers. However, among poverty populations, an internal-control orientation may reflect a lack of realism and could induce negative motivations and achievement. The individual might blame himself for failures caused by external obstacles beyond his control—namely, racial discrimination.

This study highlighted the importance of motivational factors. The work experience of the girls' parents and contacts figured greatly in their views of the world of work. Since these experiences were limited to menial and/or unskilled jobs, these were the only aspects of the world of work about which the girls were knowledgeable. With such a limited view of employment, the teenagers expressed a distaste for work and tended to discount as work those tasks that were enjoyable. The project, through the job hunt, sought to promote a realistic appraisal of the employment situation in the New York City labor market. Through discussion of their experiences in group sessions, the young women were able to separate those personal things they had to work on from those things beyond their individual responsibility. Recognition of these problems at least headed these young women in the right direction.

Attitudes Toward Seeking Employment

Although the work theme was introduced by the field staff in more than half of the first twenty-eight sessions of the Central Harlem group, the resource assistants evidenced little basic concern with the issue of employment per se. While the resource assistants were aware that the project focus was black teenage unemployment, they were not actively concerned with securing a permanent job or considering long-range career planning. Five of the Harlem resource assistants and two from the Brooklyn group had had previous work experience, mainly in jobs located in their neighborhoods. At this stage of their lives, work was viewed as occasionally necessary to meet specific current needs. This was best expressed by one of the assistants in a comment to one of the staff: "The best time for a girl to look for a job is when she needs it."

With one or two exceptions, the families of these teenagers were able to provide the necessities and some extras and thus facilitate this attitude. Married assistants realized that their situations would be improved if they aided their husbands in the support of the family. But neither married nor unmarried assistants were prepared to face the prospect of a career of work that was most likely to portend a succession of dull, low-salaried, unrewarding jobs.

Although these teenagers displayed a good deal of sophistication in understanding the availability of jobs in certain areas, they were not sanguine about their chances to secure those jobs or to anticipate rewarding ongoing job experiences in view of the effect of racial prejudice and discrimination in hiring practices and job advancement. They also anticipated that they, as young black women, would have to be wary of additional exploitative predispositions. In sum, the majority of the assistants approached the job hunt with apprehension and little expectation of success.

The group meetings and individual discussions with staff members led to the identification of the "put down" techniques which could lead to an unsuccessful completion of the job application procedure as well as protect them from a system they perceived as hostile and rejecting. In such "put downs" they were able to avoid dealing with whatever problems of inadequate preparation or unfamiliarity with the work world that inhibited their potential employment.

A minority of the assistants felt that holding jobs as adults was essential to their self-esteem. But for the most part their poverty status did not apparently increase their readiness to move into adult roles or to assume responsibility for self-support. Like most other teenagers, the assistants were primarily concerned with establishing themselves in their families, peer groups, and heterosexual relationships. Of equal significance was the unspoken acceptance of the inevitability of living out their lives in a cycle of poverty and dependence.

It is possible that, for somewhat different reasons, the behavior of black youths represents a challenging of the American work ethic similar to that being attempted by young members of white middle-class families. Certain members of the white youth culture believe that the "rat race" has not yielded a happy life for their parents or themselves, even though it has brought the material goods that they have enjoyed. Black young people have found that their parents were deprived of desirable jobs and the chance to earn high incomes in legitimate business, yet the young people have acquired the clothing and entertainments they have wanted. They see many adults in the community whose jobs provide no apparent reward other than income, and sometimes even this earned income does not place the family above the poverty line. The ghetto youth generally do not subscribe to the belief that a hard day's work is so desirable or necessary to self-esteem, since the work site might be a factory or the residence of a well-to-do family, both some distance from the neighborhood.

In a recent exploration of work attitudes, Leonard Goodwin compared responses from three groups: young black men from low-income families, young black men from higher-income backgrounds having upwardly-mobile aspirations, and suburban white youths. He found that while work was generally seen as one of the best sources of income by all three groups, it was not the sole source of achieving economic status and material wealth for the poor black teenage males.

The girls we talked with tended to be critical of jobs that provided low pay (how much is "low" varied with their knowledge of salaries) and required work in unpleasant conditions (factory work is generally undesirable). They reacted strongly against news that a program was being set up to recruit girls for office-cleaning jobs. At the same time, most of the girls indicated that they expect to work and want to work. The Harlem and Brooklyn resource assistants were asked to write on jobs they would want in the future. Their responses to the questions follow:

Question: Pretend you are working five years from now, what kind of job would you want to have? Describe.

1H: "Typist."

2H: "I hope to be a sociologist."

3H: "I plan to be a wife, a student, and on my way to becoming a good physical therapist."

4H: "Secretary, typing, steno. Working for whoever requires my secretarial work."

5H: "Telephone company—operator."

6H: "I don't know."

7H: "A bookkeeper's job. I want my job to be clean, with nice people and good pay."

8H: "I would like to be working as a nurse."

9H: "R.N., hospital."

10H: "I really can't say because I don't know as of now."

11H: "In the office, business where I can make some money."

12H: "A job paying good enough to support my family in an exciting field."

3B: "Five years from now, I would like to be doing typing work in an office."

6B: "I would like to teach first-graders."

Only two of the fourteen respondents said they did not know what kinds of jobs they would have. None of the girls challenged the situation—i.e., "pretend you are working." The staff interpreted this as an indication that all believed there is a good chance they will be working in five years or involved in pursuit of a career.

It must be realized that attitudes are shaped by knowledge of the world of work, and discussions or written exercises showed that job knowledge among this population is limited. This fact is discussed further in this chapter. A section of the questionnaire pretested by the Harlem resource assistants was devoted to identifying certain occupations and indicating the desirability of these jobs. The girls found this to be a tedious exercise; the list included a wide range of professional, skilled, and semiskilled jobs, indoor and outdoor jobs; jobs that are known by many different names. While most girls said they had heard of most of the jobs, many had difficulty explaining the duties of the workers. Stating whether a job was good or bad caused difficulty. Even girls who had an accurate understanding of the job had trouble making a choice because some were jobs for which the pay is good, but the duties

were considered undesirable or the exercise of these duties had negative connotations in their communities (judge, policeman). Another group exercise
that revealed how unfamiliar many girls were with job titles, duties and
salaries was the reading of newspaper want ads.

Despite the many negative feelings the girls have toward certain jobs, and
despite the adjustments in social patterns and time use that these girls would
have to make, it cannot be said that they are opposed to work or unwilling
to earn their income, although they might not be ready to fully support themselves. In a recent monograph on the strengths of black families, Dr. Robert
Hill of the National Urban League stresses that a strong work orientation exists
among low-income black families and that the only work incentive needed is
decent pay for decent jobs.[2] Most of the girls were eager to participate in job
hunts. Some members of the Harlem group were interested in performing as
many other small work assignments as were offered (such as light clerical work
at MARC, recruitment, and interviewing girls). Some girls selected carefully
companies they wanted to go to with the hope they really would be hired for
a job. Furthermore, while few were prepared to seek the jobs they would hold
for years to come, many showed curiosity about the world of work and readiness for jobs. All of the girls received support for their job search efforts in
the form of payment for transportation expenses, assistance with child care
arrangements, and encouragement for discussing with peers and staff their
questions and apprehensions.

A few group members had worked prior to forming the group; others
were seeking their first jobs during the project. The girls who were in school
tended to be the girls most active in seeking employment. They did not expect
to find interesting or exciting jobs, but they knew the jobs would be either
part-time or short-term. They saw their earnings as a means to purchase things
they needed now, and they looked forward to having a greater choice of jobs
in the future. It should be noted that many girls were quite savings-conscious;
during the fall months, many left their weekly group sessions payments in a
"Christmas Club" fund; the college student was known as the most frugal girl
in the Harlem group.

Assignments on job hunts and the discussions on the usefulness of the
structured questionnaires as a technique of collecting data on the sociological
and psychological processes that affect black unemployed teenage females
provided us with additional insights into the perceptions of jobs held by the
study population.

Experience in Seeking Employment

Both the Harlem and Brooklyn study groups were asked to participate
in job-seeking assignments. They were asked to apply for jobs at banks,
broadcasting companies, insurance companies, hospitals, utilities, and several

large firms in the midtown Manhattan business district. The assistants were
told to be alert to the age range and racial makeup of the staff and other job
applicants at these places of business. They were to be attentive to the kind
of reception given them, the interview and application questions, the amount
of time various parts of the application process took, and their feelings throughout the entire period. The assistants reported these experiences to staff members and discussed them at the group session. A sampling of case summaries
of such job interview experiences are cited later in this chapter.

In general the following practices seemed to characterize the interview
situation for these assistants:

1.   Their applications were accepted but seemed to have been "circular
filed" rather than entered in the active files.

2.   New qualifications were introduced to screen out the assistants.

3.   Interviewers were overtly hostile and rude with the black applicants
but not with the whites.

4.   Interviewers were prone to give advice about education and training
rather than respond directly to the assistant's job application.

Table 6-1
Companies Visited by Resource Assistants

		Location
1.	Harlem Hospital	H
2.	Manufacturers Hanover Trust	M
3.	New York Telephone Company	B&M
4.	Olsten's Temporary	M
5.	Dial Employment Agency	M
6.	Appeal Employment Agency	M
7.	Neighborhood Youth Corps	H
8.	Harlem Teams for Self-Help	H
9.	Youth in Action	B
10.	Brooklyn Adult Training Center (BATC)	B
11.	Women's Job Corps	B&H
12.	Macy's Department Store	M
13.	Abraham and Straus Department Store	B
14.	Martin's Department Store	B
15.	Chock Full O'Nuts	H
16.	Columbia-Presbyterian Medical Center	M
17.	Metropolitan Life Insurance Company	M
18.	Charles Pfizer and Company	M
19.	International Paper Company	M
20.	National Broadcasting Company (N.B.C.)	M
21.	American Broadcasting Company (A.B.C.)	M

Location code: B   Brooklyn
                  H   Harlem
                  M   Manhattan

5.   Those black applicants who were accepted for jobs were given more routine, lower-paying jobs than comparable white applicants.

Four resource assistants found jobs after either group discussions on job search or after participating in the job hunt project. From the job hunt activities one assistant found a clerical job with a business firm located outside of her neighborhood. Another assistant was hired as a file clerk one month before the termination of group sessions. A third resource assistant secured a position as a receptionist in an office where her sister was already employed. Apparently, prior to the group discussion it had not occurred to her that her sister was a resource. A part-time position as a wrapper for a large department store was obtained as a result of another assistant asking her mother about available positions in her place of work.

Case Summaries of Job Search Experiences

Case I
Applicant: Seventeen years old, 11th-year high school student.
Experience: Went to a snack restaurant chain store where friend work-
                    ed looking for a job. Manager told her that he would
                    remember her face and would contact her through her
                    friend, if necessary. The fact that he had not requested
                    her address, telephone number, or application was disturb-
                    ing to both girls.

Case II
Applicant: Seventeen years old, recently married woman with one
                    child, tenth-year high school dropout.
Experience: Approached telephone company with clerical or operator
                    job in mind. Completed application but was told by inter-
                    viewer that she would need statement from school of her
                    plans not to return. Applicant was amazed at request since
                    it was midsummer and her school was closed.

Case III
Applicant: Seventeen years old, eleventh-year high school student.
Experience: Applied for employment at telephone company. Filled out
                    application and passed aptitude test. Was asked to return
                    for interview. When applicant returned, she was congrat-
                    ulated on passing aptitude test but could not be hired
                    because she was too young and was currently attending
                    school. Applicant could not understand why she had to
                    make a second trip to hear such an outcome.

Case IV

Applicant: Seventeen years old, eleventh-year high school student.

Experience: Applied for nurse's aide job at neighborhood hospital.
                      Filled out application and passed test. Interviewer
                      informed her that she had passed test and that they would
                      call her. Hospital did not call.

Case V

Applicant: Seventeen years old, eleventh-year high school student.
                      Enrolled in the Cooperative Nursing Training Program in
                      ninth school year.

Experience: Sought summer position as a coop nurse at neighborhood
                      hospital. Interviewer informed her that before she could
                      become a paid trainee, she would have to do volunteer work
                      for a school year and to come back at the beginning of the
                      school year while she is enrolled in coop course.

Case VI

Applicant: Seventeen years old, eleventh-year high school student.

Experience: Applied for coop nurse position at a local hospital. Com-
                      pleted application form, but was told that there were no
                      such openings as coop nurse. Interviewer informed appli-
                      cant of typists openings. Applicant, however, does not
                      type.

Case VII

Applicant: Eighteen years old, freshman in college.

Experience: Applied for part-time employment at large department
                      store. Completed application. Interviewer would not hire
                      because she had never done sales before while attending
                      school and could not judge how much time she would be
                      able to devote to the job.

Case VIII

Applicant: Sixteen years old, married, mother of one, tenth-year high
                      school student.

Experience: Applied at Brooklyn department store. Told no openings
                      at that time and store would contact her when positions
                      became available.

Case IX

Applicant: Sixteen years old, married, mother of one, tenth-year high
                      school student.

Experience: Completed application at Brooklyn department store. Was told store does not hire unless applicant is eighteen and experienced.

Case X

Applicant: Two seventeen-year-olds, eleventh-year high school students.

Experience: Applied for salesgirl positions at prestigious department store. Girls noticed all employment office staff were white. Three "older" white women were also waiting to be interviewed. Everyone stared at the two girls, and they, in turn, became uncomfortable and left.

Case XI

Applicant: Seventeen years old, completed tenth-year high school, dropout.

Experience: Applied for a typist position at a national broadcasting company. Was told there were no openings at the present time. She did not fill out application nor inquire about openings in other areas.

Case XII

Applicant: Eighteen years old, mother, unmarried, school dropout.

Experience: Approached a national broadcasting company. Completed application, then waited thirty minutes for interview. Applicant saw no black staff in the office and noticed that mostly whites were applying for positions. Interviewed by middle-aged white women who told her that she did not type well enough. When applicant inquired about training program, she was told that the program was only available to those hired. Applicant then proceeded to tell interviewer about her attitude. Applicant then became angry and left when she realized she was being turned down again.

Case XIII

Applicant: Sixteen years old, unwed mother, one child, tenth-year high school student.

Experience: Applied for employment at a national broadcasting company. Was told she did not have the skills necessary for current openings.

Case XIV

Applicant: Sixteen years old, unwed mother, one child, tenth-year high school student.

Experience: Sought job at a paper company. Black receptionist gave
                       young woman an application to fill out. The receptionist
                       was polite but stared at applicant while she waited. Appli-
                       cant was youngest person applying for position. She was
                       seen by a white interviewer who inquired whether applicant
                       could type. Applicant cannot type, therefore, interviewer
                       told her there were no openings but gave her his business
                       card and told her that she would be contacted if clerical
                       position became available.

Case XV
Applicant: Seventeen years old, tenth-year high school student.
Experience: Applicant went to the New York State Employment Ser-
                       vice office. She was told, "you need to be twenty-one,
                       but go upstairs anyway." Did as she was told and was
                       asked for her zip code. Applicant was then sent to a dis-
                       trict office near her home. At this office a black represen-
                       tative told her to wait for an interview with another NYSES
                       counselor, but he did not appear.

Case XVI
Applicant: Eighteen years old, unwed mother, one child, school drop-
                       out.
Experience: Applied at an insurance company for employment. Com-
                       pleted application and was directed to interviewer. Given
                       fifteen-minute aptitude test. Test scores were accepted.
                       Interview was continued and applicant was asked of per-
                       sonal health and day care problems. Interviewer informed
                       applicant about jobs. Was told eligible for clerical jobs
                       paying $85-$95 weekly with salary increases four times
                       yearly. Applicant was then sent to medical examination.
                       Told she would hear in two weeks. Was hired but decided
                       to quit after short stay on the job.

Case XVII
Applicant: Seventeen years old, recently married, one child, tenth-year
                       high school dropout.
Experience: Applicant applied for a teller position at a neighborhood
                       bank. They told her she could not be hired because she did
                       not have high school diploma.

Case XVIII

Applicant:	Eighteen years old, married, one child, twelfth-year high school dropout, attending night school.
Experience:	Visited electric company. She was told after she had been interviewed and tested that only high school graduates could be accepted for jobs.

Case XIX

Applicant:	Sixteen years old, married, one child, tenth-year high school student.
Experience:	Applied for position at an insurance company. Was informed that the company only hires high school seniors for part-time positions.

Case XX

Applicant:	Eighteen years old, married, one child, twelfth-year high school dropout, attending night school.
Experience:	Registered as a file clerk who can do light typing with a temporary employment agency. Applicant took a typing test. Talked with interviewer who assured her she would be placed. Applicant has not been placed as yet.

Case XXI

Applicant:	Seventeen years old, eleventh-year high school student.
Experience:	Inquired about two apparently identical airline receptionist jobs at two different (private) employment agencies.

Agency A: Interviewer did not appear interested in applicant. Applicant was told she could not be hired.

Agency B: Interviewer encouraged applicant to return to school and return to agency to apply for a job when she received her high school diploma.

Case XXII

Applicant:	Eighteen years old, married, one child, twelfth-year high school dropout, attending night school.
Experience:	Male employee of a private employment agency took one look at applicant and said his company could not help her. She felt this man's reaction meant, "We don't need any more black girls."

Case XXIII
Applicant: Eighteen years old, high school senior planning to go to
                        college.
Experience: Applied for a position at a pharmaceutical company. She
                        was told she could not be given any information about
                        jobs until application was filled out and processed. The
                        personnel staff was polite. Received letter informing her
                        that there were no positions open, but she would be
                        contacted when one came up.

   Throughout the project, resource assistants were asked to relate facts and
impressions of their experience with the world of work and training. Some of
these experiences occurred prior to participation in the project.

Resource Assistant: Eighteen years old, unwed mother, tenth-grade dropout.
Experience and   Resource assistant secured a position through the job search
Comments: procedure. She was being trained to operate a calculator at
                         an insurance company. Resource assistant advised others
                         not to get a job. She reported that it costs too much and
                         claimed she had to borrow money to go to work because
                         her paycheck was held until the end of her second week on
                         the job.

Resource Assistant: Sixteen years old, unwed mother, tenth-year high school
                         student.
Experience and   Resource assistant did not consider her duties at a dry
Comments: cleaners establishment a "job," because she only worked
                         two hours a day and the place was "right downstairs"
                         (from where she resides). Furthermore, she was paid
                         only $1.25 per hour. Resource assistant considered a
                         position she held as a switchboard operator at $2.05 per
                         hour a "job."

Resource Assistant: Seventeen years old, eleventh-year high school student.
Experience and   Resource assistant advised others never to work at a local
Comments: chain snack bar. She had worked there and reported the
                         constant rush, very talkative or demanding customers,
                         and attitude of older union member coworkers as things
                         that made the job particularly taxing at times. She stated
                         that she would never take a job where she could not take
                         a coffee break.

| Resource Assistant: | Nineteen years old, unwed mother, ninth-year high school dropout, attended night school and Brooklyn Adult Training Center. |
| Experience and Comments: | In her own opinion, resource assistant is a self-confident, strong-minded girl. She admitted to being quite nervous about having interviews and taking tests. |

Employment Problems

Many themes emerged which help to categorize the employment problems of young people.

Systematic Societal Impediments

The hostility and rejection that the black female teenagers of the study group consistently anticipated actually pervaded their job-seeking activities because of the following societal impediments:

1. Among public employment and training agencies the needs of teenage girls are given low priority. This is manifest in several ways: no provision is made for them, whether because of their youth or sex, e.g., programs in "male trades"; counselors may not refer young teenagers to those programs that provide for female applicants. The coordination of employment resources by agencies within the target areas was hampered by inefficiency due to insufficient budgets, administrative conflicts, and excessive work loads, such that any additional client was another too many.

2. The advertised equal opportunity hiring practices of the private business and public utilities sector remain at variance with a number of their actual screening procedures for potential employees. These often involve requirements that seem straightforward enough when explained; their execution, however, reveals them as dead-end exercises (see Case Summaries of Job Search Experiences, Cases III, XII, XVIII, and XXIII).

3. The unskilled, black female teenager, whether in school or out, whether single, married, or unwed mother, is generally regarded as a "poor employment risk."

4. There are legal and official company policy barriers which restrict young teenagers in the labor market. Until they reach eighteen, young people must obtain working papers. Some companies simply will not accept people under eighteen or under twenty-one. Educational requirements and programs designed for males only or welfare families only also limit the choices of the young poor black female.

5.   Public schools that should provide links to the world of work fail to do so. Any channels that do exist are overburdened and complicated by bureaucracy.

6.   Given the large proportion of young mothers in the black community and the fact that many black teenage girls live in households with small children, the issue of day care must be considered.

Day Care

A recent study concludes that the provision of free and adequate day care services to low-income mothers would lead to an increase in their labor force participation of about ten percentage points (from 32 percent to 42 percent). In 1970 on a national basis, mothers in poverty were generally less likely to be in the labor force than nonpoor mothers. Also, the more years of education a mother has, the more likely she is to be in the labor force. The lowest participation within the given educational and age ranges are found among mothers with children under three years of age. The young mothers in our study group may be deterred from increased labor force participation by age of child, and the role burdens of mother.[3]

Eight members from the combined study groups had at least one child, and six of these young mothers had some work experience. (See table 6-2 and figure 6-1.) Child care in New York City is a monumental problem for many mothers who would like either to work or to continue their education. In a recent study conducted by the Bureau of Labor Statistics, one out of four mothers could not find babysitters or day care at a price they could afford to pay. Other difficulties, such as lack of day care within walking distance of the home, inconvenient transportation arrangements, and the inadequate capacity of day care centers are deterring factors for women with children who wish to enter the work force or educational and/or training programs.[4]

During 1971 in New York City, there were 934 day care services in operation with a total of 46,190 registered children.[5] Family care services, which accommodate children from two to six years of age in groups of six or more in a home environment, encompass such diverse sponsors as community groups, churches, government, hospitals, and colleges. Family Day Care Services enroll an additional 6054 preschoolers. Infant Day Care, the newest of the services, has thirteen programs which care for 210 children under two years of age. Finally, there are forty-seven institutions, mainly shelters, with child care programs.

Even with this impressive array of services, New York City is faced with the problems of disorganization and inadequate facilities. It has been estimated that more than 100,000 children could benefit from expanded day care facilities, yet lack of funds and red tape discourage new centers. For instance, there are

Table 6-2
Work Experience of Study Group Members with Children

Group Member	Pre-Project	During-Project	Post-Project
1H		X	
2H			
3H			
4H	X		
5H			
6H			
7H			
8H	X		X
9H			
10H			
11H			
12H		X	
1B			
2B			
3B			
4B	X	X	X
5B			
6B			
7B			
8B		X	X
Total	3	4	3

Source: Project data, 1970-71.

twenty-five or more regulations regarding group size, composition staff, medical care, outside consultation, and even the dimensions of diaper-changing tables. Then, there is the licensing hurdle; in order to acquire a license, a center must be approved by at least four different agencies: the Department of Health Day Care Division, Buildings Department, Fire Department, and the Department of Social Services. Finally, whereas the national figure for day care per child is $2000 per year; in New York City the costs can jump to $2500 or $3000 annually.

In response to problems such as these, a big step in the right direction was taken on July 1, 1971 when New York City became the first city to institute an Agency for Child Development. This agency brings together all preschool programs with the exceptions of the Board of Education's prekindergarten program for 12,000 children, and the Recreation and Parks Department's preschool program for 3000 children.

The greater needs of low-income mothers and those who need day care the most are still not being met by day care programs. In 1971 when New York State ordered a change in day care fees, New York City refused to institute the

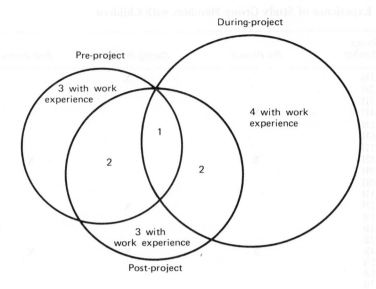

Figure 6-1. Work Experience of Study Group Members with Children

new fees on the grounds that the working poor and middle classes would be excluded and that day care centers would become ghettos for the very poor. The new fee scale of 50 cents to $16.50 a week would have been lower than the prevailing $2.00 to $25.00 a week, but the income standards also would be altered so that about 10 percent of the 20,000 children now in city centers would no longer be eligible for state support. For these children the fees would jump as high as $27.50 a week. This would penalize parents who would rather work than go on welfare.[6]

The Department of Social Services and the Family Day Care programs operate from eight in the morning to six at night. Other public programs operate only a half day. In the Central Harlem area there are approximately twenty-four licensed day care centers.[7] Of those twenty-four centers, only one has no fees, one is on a scholarship basis only, and sixteen of the centers are on a sliding-scale payment plan. None of the centers listed offered any infant care, the youngest age being two. Most programs are for children between ages of three and six. No center has any programs for children above age nine.

Most of the programs do not offer transportation for children between home and the center; those that do charge extra for this service. Another area of great need is day care for handicapped or retarded children. In Central Harlem there are no centers for retarded children and none for the handicapped.

Most of the existing day care centers have long waiting lists. It is customary to place a child on a waiting list when he is born, so that by the time the child reaches three he will have a place in a day care center.

In Central Harlem there are twenty-five Head Start programs which service about 525 children.[8] The Head Start program is not intended to provide day care services, but many times it turns out to do just that. Head Start programs do not charge any fees, and for welfare mothers there is no requirement that they work if they send their children to Head Start. Welfare recipients get first preference, and other families must meet the poverty income levels. Head Start even as a day care facility operates only half a day.

Bedford-Stuyvesant in comparison to Central Harlem has only five day care centers serving 305 children. All of the centers operate on sliding-scale payment schedules, all have summer sessions, and none offers any transportation between home and the center. These day care centers tend to be larger than the ones in Central Harlem; each center has a capacity of about fifty-five or ninety children as compared to Harlem centers that have capacities of thirty or forty children. Head Start in Bedford-Stuyvesant services about 375 children.[9]

A study conducted in the twelfth district of Brooklyn found that most women use unlicensed day care services that range from unlicensed day care centers to makeshift arrangements with a neighbor or relative. In many situations where a relative lives close by, the children will stay with relatives during the week while the mother works, and they will spend the weekends at home. Often mothers will take turns looking after each other's children. In many instances day care makeshift arrangements are achieved by having an older child take on the responsibilities for younger sisters and brothers, leaving the child to look after himself until the mother comes home from work.

Currently there is considerable debate over day care in the Federal government. In December 1971, the president vetoed the Comprehensive Child Development Bill (S. 2003). This bill would have instituted a nationwide network of public day care centers for everyone—welfare families, the working poor, and the middle class.

Dysfunctional Reference Groups Among Unemployed Black Female Teenagers

Most of the employed persons with whom the sample group came in contact work in service or unskilled jobs. Consequently, most members of the group lacked even a rudimentary knowledge of the world of work, its range and requirements. This is reflected in the related staff findings:

1. Parents and other adults in the community usually have had limited contact with the world of work, with current job-seeking approaches and manpower development programs, and with the unions and employers who are interested in hiring young people. Those parents who are aware of these channels probably have little "pull" with the organizations.

2.   There was no knowledge of minimum wage and fair labor standards.

3.   Labor unions were viewed as part of the system; there are no "advocates" for the employee. (One group session was spent discussing the union problems of the mother of a resource assistant.)

4.   There was no knowledge of the need for supervisors or standards of work execution.

5.   No distinction was made between a profession and its other professional or semiprofessional subgroups, e.g., registered nurse, practical nurse, nurse's aide.

6.   There was little appreciation of the hierarchy of formal organizations, e.g., the simple status difference between a stock clerk and receptionist.

7.   There was insufficient awareness of the nature of progression and training required to reach a goal; one assistant, for example, who had dropped out of school due to pregnancy, was placed in a clerical position, was being trained in the use of calculators, and left after two and one-half weeks.

The work experiences, both negative and positive, of the parents of these teenagers strongly affected the work attitudes of the children. Many black adult workers have experienced exceedingly high rates of unemployment even during periods of economic prosperity. Underemployment and concentration in low-wage jobs have produced great disparities in economic status of many urban blacks.

In 1972, 43 percent of all black children lived in families where the father was absent, unemployed, or out of the labor force. Median family income in 1971 was $8590 for black husband-wife families with children under eighteen years of age and $3673 for black families with female head.[10] In his social-psychological study of work orientations of the poor, Goodwin concludes:

> The picture that emerges is one of black welfare women who want to work but who, because of continuing failure in the work world, tend to become more accepting of welfare and less inclined to try again. . . . The data suggest that poor black mothers have a substantial influence on the work orientations of their sons, including those measuring acceptability of welfare and lack of confidence, and that the sons' adherence to these two orientations may lead to both early school dropout and low work activity. Hence stringent work requirements for welfare mothers, which are likely to lead to additional experience of failures, can psychologically damage not only the mothers but also their children.[11]

Individual Motivation

Closely related to this was the eventual recognition that members of the group had unique perceptions of what a job or work was. In view of their community and family experience, a "job" had essentially negative connotations. Therefore, an assistant might not report that she had "worked" if she had done something she enjoyed. One assistant was employed selling artifacts at an Afro stand; she did not consider this work, however, because she liked it and it provided her an opportunity to meet boys. One can only anticipate the dilemma to be faced by such a young woman if the demands and routine of such an activity begin to interfere with her "liking it."

Equally unique was the manner in which some of the assistants discounted jobs secured through friends and community contacts, or those with minimal pay or irregular hours. Since these kinds of jobs are the usual points of entry to the world of work, this disposition is highly problematic.

As within any population, there was a diversity of attitudes and expectations regarding different jobs. Some girls were more interested in money than in the character of the job (a major debate arose around the issue of whether to accept a domestic or custodial job). Some girls wanted to develop special talents and skills and to use these in their work. This was true of girls interested in secretarial work, commercial art, and those who felt they were good at numbers and were attracted to jobs in computer fields. Other girls expressed major interest in independence, freedom from direction and routine, while others sought careers in which they would help others (such as nursing or community work).

Much has been hypothesized recently about the effect of alternative sources of income from the subeconomy of the ghetto. In his study of employment problems of minority male youth, Bullock highlights the importance of illegal economic activity in drugs in the poor neighborhoods of Los Angeles.[12] Ferman has examined the structural solution of the ghetto and has suggested that the survival skills in the ghetto may be an important underpinning of the irregular economy by making shifts to the regular economy difficult.[13] We speculate in this study that the alternatives of illegal and illicit activities in the ghetto may be greater for young males than for young women sixteen to nineteen. Members of the study group were aware of most of the activities of the shadow economy but accepted them as just another dimension of their environment. As they moved into adult roles a precarious balance was maintained on which hangs their effective participation in training and employment. Evidence of the aging process is provided in both the lower unemployment rates and higher labor force participation rates of slightly older black women. There are no supporting data from which to conclude that large numbers of young black women are involved in the illegal and illicit activities of their communities.

Adjustments Necessary

Closely related to the section on Dysfunctional Reference Groups are the problems of entering and adjusting to first jobs.

1. Being the first, or one of a few working members of a household or group of friends, forces the young person to become independent, break ties, and make adjustments at a time in ones life when this is not easy.

2. Convincing parents that holding a job is possible at this time is difficult. Some parents fear that the attraction of earning money will cause loss of interest in school; others put the household responsibilities they have assigned their daughters above the young person's decision to work.

3. Some parent-daughter conflicts arise over if or how much of her earnings the young person should turn over to the head of household.

4. Learning the working person's routine-planning time, travelling and company customs may be difficult for a young person with no helpful adults to talk to at home and with seemingly hostile coworkers. Young black teenagers are often dismayed by the number of middle-aged white coworkers they have.

5. Financial arrangements may pose problems. Many young people are unfamiliar with budgeting and taxation. Girls who had not saved money prior to beginning a job reported they had to borrow to buy clothing, take care of carfare, lunch, and sometimes baby care.

Age and lack of experience or skills were the most prominent problems confronting the study group members in job search. The fifteen young women who had ever looked for a job reported that they had been turned down due to age, lack of skills, training or experience, lack of high school diploma or too little education, no openings, inability to accept full-time employment, interview process never completed, and prejudice on part of interviewer.

Minimum Wages

There has been a debate within the last year over whether dual minimum wage (i.e., youth differential) would reduce unemployment among young

Reasons for not Securing Employment

Reason	Number
Age	10
Lack of skills, training, or experience	8
Lack of high school diploma or too little education	4
No openings	5
Inability to accept full-time employment	1
Interview process not completed	1
Prejudiced interview	1
Total Responses	30

workers. New York City white-collar employers do not perceive young black women from low-income neighborhoods as the most attractive or preferred job applicants. It is likely that a wage differential would have a negligible impact on their employment. The employer estimates the cost of training and the disruption to the regular work force and may determine that the marginal cost of hiring is greater than marginal revenue product. Folk indicated in his investigation of youth unemployment that employers have become more selective—preferring older to younger youth and white to nonwhite.[14]

Employers will not hire and train disadvantaged black workers unless some kind of subsidy is given to them. Daniel Holland has recently evaluated differences between tax credits to business firms versus direct subsidies as an incentive to promote on-the-job training and employment of the hard-core disadvantaged. Extra costs of dislocations, conflicts, frictions, and disruptions that are measured in tension, lowered productivity, and necessary increases in supervisory responsibilities may place the disadvantaged worker at a comparative disadvantage with standard workers (no training costs need be incurred). Holland prefers the contractual subsidies because hard-core disadvantaged may require considerable training and through training will be able to fill primary job slots. However, economic incentives, even if seemingly generous, may not alone insure the success of programs designed to train and employ the disadvantaged.[15]

The changes in attitude toward the work world and ability to manipulate the "system" that the study group members gained through project participation may not be *immediately* exhibited in each of the twenty young women. One girl expressed that the project had given her the extra push she needed to search for a job. She accepted a job toward the end of the project period. Another young woman mentioned that she appreciated the group sessions as an opportunity for discussions and advice on personal as well as employment matters. A third study group member who found a job as a result of the job hunt activity, which was her initial contact with the world of work, complained during the first few weeks of her employment that it costs too much to work. She had to borrow money to get to work since her paycheck was held until the end of the second week on the job. This young woman quit her job during the project. However, toward the end of the project, she regretted not having taken advantage of the job and reapplied for her old job, but was told that there were no openings. She continued to look for work. Another young woman was quite proud of having found her first full-time job during the job hunt period. A Brooklyn group member who secured full-time employment after attending four group sessions stated that she wished she had known of the existence of the group earlier because the discussion concerning work would have been helpful to her. The job hunt activity produced confidence in searching for a job in a midtown office area for another young woman. After the end of the field work, the staff continued to communicate with both the Harlem and the Brooklyn study groups.

Post-Project Employment Status, 1972

As of March 1972, five of the Harlem group members were working. Two had reentered the educational system, and one was enrolled in a community program. A brief description of the twelve Harlem group members' training or post-employment status is as follows:

1H is currently working part-time as a salesclerk in one of the large downtown department stores. Her hourly wage is $2.05. 1H did not complete her participation at the New York Adult Training Center. She had been referred to the center by Harlem Teams for Self-Help, where she completed a basic education course. Before enrolling in the Harlem Teams program, 1H was employed as a receptionist in a fabric firm. She discontinued working to participate in the Harlem Teams basic education program.

2H is working part-time as a saleswoman in a large department store at $2.00 an hour. She is also working part-time as a clerk at Hunter College, where she is enrolled as a freshman. Her wage at the college is $1.85 per hour. 2H's academic goal is to earn a Ph.D. in sociology. 2H uses her earnings toward her school expenses.

3H is employed as a cashier at $2.25 an hour at one of the large downtown department stores. She is working part-time while in her second year of college. 3H previously worked as a cashier at a men's clothing store.

4H has reentered the educational system. She is enrolled in night school. During the summer of 1971, 4H participated in the Economic Manpower Training Program. She entered this program from the WIN program and was referred by the Department of Social Services. 4H has had very limited work experience.

5H is not in school nor is she participating in a training program or working. She had previously worked as a salesclerk at an Afro-stand.

6H is not in training, school, or working.

7H has reentered the educational system. She is attending night school. During the summer months, she worked as a cashier and packer in a local grocery store. She had worked in the same store before and reapplied when the Manpower Project ended.

8H is employed on a part-time basis as a dietary aide in a hospital. Her hourly wage is $3.20. She was employed in the same capacity on a full-time basis during the summer of 1971. 8H is a day student in high school. Previously, she had worked as an operator with the telephone company and in a cleaning establishment.

9H is working part-time in the post office. This is her first job.

10H is not involved in a training, educational, or employment situation. During the summer of 1971, she worked as a clerk in the post office. The summer before, she was employed by the Neighborhood Youth Corps in its Narcotics Program.

11H is a senior in high school. For the last two summers, she has worked as a waitress at a snackbar chain in one of the midtown stores. She has been offered a similar position with more pay in her neighborhood, but her mother would not allow 11H to accept it. The mother was afraid for her daughter because there was too much hustling in the area.

12H is involved in the CHANCE Program and participated in its home economics course. The course teaches welfare recipients how to manage money and cook a balanced meal. 12H had found employment through the job search procedure. She later quit the job. However, toward the end of the project, she announced that she regretted having quit her position and had returned to the company to apply for another. At this time, however, there were no openings. 12H stated that she would continue looking for a job.

Conclusion

Few of the resource assistants had considerable work experience prior to participation in the group. Nevertheless, they indicated that they expected to work and wanted to work. Some of the resource assistants believed that racial discrimination would bar them from securing good jobs. In addition, they anticipated attempts of sexual exploitation on the work site. Several girls had experienced such exploitation on previous jobs. As a result, they were inclined to use a "put down" technique—not initiating or completing job search proceduces in order to shield themselves from expected rejection and hostility.

The girls possessed rudimentary knowledge of the world of work. They were unfamiliar with corresponding job titles, duties, required training, and salaries. They had unique perceptions of what a job is. Jobs frequently had a negative connotation. Work experience that was enjoyed or had been found through family or friends, or which paid the minimum wage was not likely to be considered as a job. Resource assistants with small children were not able to find satisfactory child care arrangements. Both Central Harlem and Bedford-Stuyvesant lacked an adequate number of day care facilities.

Both Harlem and Brooklyn study groups participated in job-seeking assignments. They applied for various positions in twenty-one companies. The resource assistants were asked to report their experiences on the job hunts. The practices the resource assistants encountered were: there applications were accepted but not entered in the active files, credential barriers were set up, interviewers were overtly hostile and rude to black interviewees, interviewers advised applicants on training and education rather than informing them of current job openings, and black applicants accepted for jobs were given lower status and paying positions than comparable whites. Nevertheless, by the end of the project, eight of the Harlem group members had found permanent or summer jobs, or enrolled in training programs.

Field testing of several of the findings of this investigation should be

extensive enough to include some measure of the relationships between the level
of involvement in the peer group and the success and failure of these young
women during the first year following the peer group network. Perhaps the
labor market entry can be facilitated for young black women from low-income
families by undergirding and carefully nurturing those strengths which they
exhibit as they move into adulthood.

Notes

Chapter 2
Findings and Recommendations

1. Sally Hillsman Baker, "Entry Into the Labor Market: The Preparation and Job Placement of Negro and White Vocational High School Graduates" (Ph. D. Dissertation, Columbia University, 1970).
2. *The Job Crisis for Black Youth*: Report of the Twentieth Century Fund Task Force on Employment Problems of Black Youth, with a Background Paper by Sar A. Levitan and Robert Taggart (New York: Praeger, 1971), p. 12. © 1971 by the Twentieth Century Fund, New York.

Chapter 3
Introduction

1. The poverty area classification was developed by the US Bureau of the Census for the Office of Economic Opportunity. Poverty areas were determined by ranking census tracks in metropolitan areas with a 1960 population of 250,000 or more according to the relative presence of each of the following equally weighted poverty-linked characteristics: (1) families with money incomes below $3000; (2) children under eighteen years old not living with both parents; (3) persons twenty-five years and over with less than eight years of school completed; (4) unskilled males (laborers and service workers) in the civilian labor force; and (5) housing units dilapidated or lacking some or all plumbing facilities. The designated low-income areas have been revised to reflect more recent socioeconomic data and the views of local knowledgeable agencies.
2. Charles C. Holt, et al., *The Unemployment-Inflation Dilemma: A Manpower Solution* (Washington, D.C.: The Urban Institute, 1971).
3. US Department of Labor, Bureau of Labor Statistics, *Employment of School-Age Youth, October 1971.* Special Labor Force Report 147, Table C, p. A-10.
4. US Department of Labor, Bureau of Labor Statistics, *Some Facts Relating to the New York Scene* (New York: Bureau of Labor Statistics, Middle Atlantic Regional Office, 1971).
5. Bernard Goldstein, *Low Income Youth in Urban Areas: A Critical Review of the Literature* (New York: Holt, Rinehart and Winston, 1967).

6. Camile Jeffers, *Living Poor: A Participant Observer Study of Priorities and Choices* (Ann Arbor, Mich.: Ann Arbor Publishers, 1967), and Hylan Lewis, "Culture, Class and Family Life Among Low Income Urban Negroes," in *Employment, Race, and Poverty*, ed. by Arthur M. Ross and Herbert Hill (New York: Harcourt, Brace and World, 1967).

7. Elizabeth Herzog, *About the Poor: Some Facts and Some Factors* (Washington, D.C.: Department of Health, Education, and Welfare, SRS, Children's Bureau, 1967).

8. Kenneth B. Clark, *Dark Ghetto: Dilemmas of Social Power* (New York: Harper and Row, 1967), p. 34.

Chapter 5
The Study Groups and Their Communities

1. Edward C. Burks, "Growth of Poverty in City Creating New Poor Zones," *New York Times*, April 10, 1972, p. 40.

2. US Department of Labor, Bureau of Labor Statistics, *The Economics of Working and Living in New York City* (New York: Middle Atlantic Region, 1972), p. 27; US Department of Labor, *Manpower Report of the President* (Washington, D.C.: Government Printing Office, 1972), p. 78.

3. US Department of Labor, *The Economics of Working and Living in New York City*, p. 26.

4. *Ibid.*, p. 13.

5. New York City Planning Commission, *Planning for Jobs* (New York: New York City Planning Commission, 1971), p. 10.

6. US Department of Labor, Bureau of Labor Statistics, *Sub-Employment in the Slums of New York* (Washington, D.C.: Government Printing Office, 1966).

7. US Department of Labor, Bureau of Labor Statistics, *Poverty Area Profiles: Characteristics of the Unemployed*, Regional Report No. 14 (New York: US Department of Labor, Bureau of Labor Statistics, 1970), p. 19.

8. US Department of Labor, *The Economics of Working and Living in New York City*, p. 33.

9. US Department of Labor, Bureau of Labor Statistics, *Poverty Area Profiles: Working Age Nonparticipants; Persons Not in the Labor Force and Their Employment Problems*, Regional Report No. 22 (New York: US Department of Labor, Bureau of Labor Statistics, 1971).

10. Peter B. Doeringer and Michael J. Piore, *Internal Labor Markets and Manpower Analysis* (Lexington, Mass.: D.C. Heath and Co., 1971), p. 165.

11. Economic Development Council of New York City, Inc., *New York City's Publicly-Financed Manpower Programs—Structure and Function* (New York, 1970), p. 2.

12. Sally Hillsman Baker, "Entry Into the Labor Market: The Preparation and Job Placement of Negro and White Vocational High School Graduates" (Ph.D. Dissertation, Columbia University, 1970), p. 110.

13. Community Service Society of New York, Committee on Youth and Correction, *Occupational Education and Training in Our High Schools, Findings and Recommendations* (New York: Community Service Society of New York, 1971), p. 5.

14. Howard Hayghe, *Employment of High School Graduates and Dropouts,* Special Labor Force Report No. 121 (Washington, D.C.: US Department of Labor, 1970), p. 38.

15. "Heroin Addiction and Drug Abuse in New York," *City Almanac* 6; 6 (1972), p. 4.

16. Phyllis A. Wallace, "Employment Status of Black Women" (research in progress).

17. Ray Marshall, "Trends in Black Income and Employment," *The AFL-CIO American Federationist* 78:7 (1971), p. 1

18. Phyllis A. Wallace, "Economics and the Values of Society" from *Proceedings of the 1971 Invitational Conference on Testing Problems—Educational Change: Implications for Measurement* (Princeton, N.J.: Educational Testing Service, 1971), p. 32. All rights reserved, Reprinted by permission.

Chapter 6
Employment Problems of Black Teenage Females

1. Gerald Gurin, *Inner-City Negro Youth in a Job Training Project* (Ann Arbor: University of Michigan, Institute for Social Research, 1968).

2. Robert B. Hill, *The Strengths of Black Families* (New York: Emerson Hall Publishers, Inc,, 1971), p. 14.

3. US Office of Economic Opportunity, Office of Planning Research and Evaluation, *A Study of Day Care's Effect on the Labor Force Participation of Low-Income Mothers* (Washington, D.C., 1973).

4. US Department of Labor, Bureau of Labor Statistics, *Poverty Area Profiles: Working Age Nonparticipants; Persons Not in the Labor Force and Their Employment Problems*, Regional Report No. 22 (New York: US Department of Labor, Bureau of Labor Statistics, 1971).

5. New York City Bureau of Child Health, Division of Day Care, Day Camps and Institutions, "Day Care Services in Operation—December 1971." (Mimeographed.)

6. Maurice Carroll, "City Hall Hearing Is Converted Into a Day Care Center Scene," *New York Times*, July 21, 1971, p. 41.

7. *Directory of Day Care Services in New York City* (New York: Department of Health, New York City, 1971).

8. *Ibid.*

9. *Ibid.*

10. Anne M. Young, "Children of Working Mothers," US Department of Labor, Bureau of Labor Statistics, *Monthly Labor Review*, April 1973, p. 39.

11. Leonard Goodwin, *Do the Poor Want to Work*? (Washington, D.C.: The Brookings Institution, 1972), pp. 113 and 115. © 1972 by the Brookings Institution, Washington, D.C.

12. Paul Bullock, *Aspiration vs. Opportunity: Careers in the Inner City* (Ann Arbor: University of Michigan-Wayne State University, Institute of Labor and Industrial Relations, 1973).
13. Louise Ferman, "The Irregular Economy" (unpublished manuscript).
14. Hugh Folk, "The Problems of Youth Unemployment," *The Transition from School to Work* (Princeton: Princeton University, 1968).
15. Daniel M. Holland, "An Evaluation of Tax Incentives for On-the-job Training of the Disadvantaged," *The Bell Journal of Economics and Management Science* 2, no. 1 (Spring 1971).

Bibliography

Adams, E. Sherman. "Coping with Ghetto Unemployment." *Conference Board Record*, May 1970, pp. 41-45.

Amos, William, and Jean Grambs, eds. *Counseling the Disadvantaged Youth.* Englewood Cliffs, N.Y.: Prentice-Hall, 1968.

Ashenfelter, Orley. "Minority Employment Patterns, 1966." A paper prepared for the United States Equal Employment Opportunity Commission and the Office of Manpower Policy Evaluation and Research of the United States Department of Labor, Princeton University, Princeton, N.J., April 1968.

Astin, Helen S. *Personal and Environmental Factors in Career Decisions of Young Women.* Washington, D.C.: Bureau of Social Science Research, Inc., 1970.

Baker, Priscilla A. "Aides Stretch Manpower in Human Services." *Occupational Outlook Quarterly* 13:4 (Winter 1969).

Baker, Sally Hillsman. "Entry Into the Labor Market: The Preparation and Job Placement of Negro and White Vocational High School Graduates." Ph.D. dissertation, Columbia University, 1970.

Barnett, Minnak. "Being a Member of a Minority Group: Relevancy and Opportunity in the World of Work." *Poverty, Education, and Race Relations: Studies and Proposals.* Edited by William C. Kvaraceus, John S. Gibson, and Thomas J. Curtin. Boston: Allyn and Bacon, 1967.

Bedger, Jean E. *Unwed Mothers: Report on Services, Financial and Client Date for 1969.* Chicago: Florence Crittenton Association of America, Inc., 1970.

Bernstein, Saul. *Alternatives to Violence: Alienated Youths and Riots, Race and Poverty.* New York: Associated Press, 1967.

Billingsley, Andrew. *Black Families in White America.* Englewood Cliffs, N.J.: Prentice-Hall, 1968.

Bolino, August C. *Manpower and the City.* Cambridge, Mass.: Schenkman Publishing Co., 1969.

Borus, Michael E. "The Economic Effectiveness of Retraining the Unemployed: A Study of the Benefits and Costs of Retraining the Unemployed Based on the Experience of Workers in Connecticut." Research Report to the Federal Reserve Bank of Boston, June 1966.

Borus, Michael, et al. "A Benefit Cost Analysis of the Neighborhood Youth Corps: The Out-of-School Program in Indiana," *Journal of Human Resources* 5:2 (1970), 139–59.

Bowen, William, and T. Aldrich Finegan. *The Economics of Labor Force Participation.* Princeton: Princeton University Press, 1969.

Bowman, Paul H., and Matthews, Charles V. *Motivations of Youth for Leaving School.* Chicago: University of Chicago Press, 1960.

Brown, Carol A. "The Expansion of Health Services." *Manpower Strategy for the Metropolis.* Edited by Eli Ginzberg and the Conservation of Human Resources Staff of Columbia University. New York: Columbia University Press, 1968.

Brozen, Yale. "The Effect of Statutory Minimum Wage Increases on Teen-age Employment." *Journal of Law and Economics* (April 1969), 109-22.

Bullock, Paul. *Aspiration vs. Opportunity: "Careers" in the Inner City.* Ann Arbor: Institute of Labor and Industrial Relations, University of Michigan-Wayne State University, 1972.

Cain, Glenn G. "Unemployment and Labor Force Participation of Secondary Workers." *Industrial Relations Review,* January 1967.

Carbine, Michael. "Communicating with the Disadvantaged." *Manpower* 1 (October 1969), 2-6.

Carroll, Stephen J., and Anthony H. Pascal, *Youth and Work: Toward a Model of Lifetime Economic Prospects.* Memorandum RM-5891-OEO. Santa Monica: The RAND Corporation, 1969.

Cassell, Frank H. "Realities and Opportunities in the Development of Jobs." *Business and Society,* Spring 1968, pp. 21-31.

Center for Studies in Vocational and Technical Education. *Research in Vocational and Technical Education: Proceedings of a Conference.* Madison: University of Wisconsin, 1966.

"Changing Status of Negro Women Workers." *Monthly Labor Review* 87 (June 1964), 671-73.

Child Welfare League of America, Inc. *Standards for Day Care Service.* New York: Child Welfare League of America, Inc., 1969.

Chopin, Eli E., ed. *Manpower Policies for Youth.* New York: Columbia University Press, 1966.

Clark, Dennis, and Abraham Wolf. *Dialect Remediation Project. Final Report.* Philadelphia: Center for Community Studies, Temple University and Berean Institute, 1966.

Clark, Kenneth B. "The Negro and the Urban Crisis." *Agenda for the Nation.* Edited by Kermit Gordon. Washington, D.C.: Brookings Institution, 1968.

———. "Education of the Minority Poor—The Key to the War on Poverty." *The Disadvantaged Poor: Education and Employment.* Washington, D.C.: Chamber of Commerce, Task Force on Economic Growth and Opportunity, 1966.

———. *Dark Ghetto: Dilemmas of Social Power.* New York: Harper and Row, 1965.

———, ed. *Youth in the Ghetto, A Study of the Consequences of Powerlessness and a Blueprint for Change.* New York: Harlem Youth Opportunities Unlimited Inc., 1964.

Cohen, Eli E., Marcia K. Freedman, Judith G. Benjamin, Seymour Lesh, and Edith F. Lynton. *Getting Hired, Getting Trained: A Study of Industry Practices and Policies on Youth Employment.* New York: National Committee on Employment of Youth, 1964.

Cohen, Malcolm S. "Married Women in the Labor Force: An Analysis of Participation Roles." *Monthly Labor Review* (October 1969) :33.

Coleman, James D. *Adolescent Society*. New York: Free Press, 1961.

Committee for Economic Development. *Improving the Public Welfare System*.
New York: Committee for Economic Development, 1970.

Corwin, R. David. *New Workers in the Banking Industry: A Minority Report*.
New York: New York University, Department of Sociology, 1970.

David, Jay, ed. *Growing Up Black*. New York: Pocket Books Edition, 1969.

Davis, Ethelyn. "Careers as Concerns of Blue-Collar Girls." *Blue-Collar World:
Studies of the American Worker*. Edited by Arthur B. Shostak and William
Gomberg. Englewood Cliffs, N.J.: Prentice-Hall, 1964.

Day Care and Child Development Council of America, Inc. *Child Care Provi-
sions in the Family Assistance Act as Passed by the House of Representatives, April 16, 1970. Bill No. H.R. 16311. Report No. 91-904*. Washington, D.C.: Day Care and Child Development Council of America, Inc.,
1970.

————. "Questions and Answers on the Child Care Provision of the Family
Assistance Act of 1969 from the United States Department of Health,
Education and Welfare." *Legislative Summary #111: Family Assistance
Act of 1969. H.R. 14173, S. 2986*. Washington, D.C.: Day Care and
Child Development Council of America, Inc., 1970, pp. 38-42.

Denman, Anne Smith. "Cultural Differences and Attitudes Toward Employment." *The Social Sciences and Manpower Research*. Iowa City: Iowa
State University, Industrial Relations Center, 1969, pp. 83-94.

Dentler, Robert A., and Mary Ellen Warshauer. *Big City Dropouts and Illiterates*.
New York: Center for Urban Education, 1965.

Dernburg, Thomas, and Kenneth Strand. "Hidden Unemployment, 1953-62: A
Quantitative Analysis by Age and Sex." *American Economic Review*,
March 1966, pp. 71-95.

Dittman, Laura L., ed. *Early Child Care: The New Perspective*. New York:
Atherton, 1968.

Doeringer, Peter B., and Michael J. Piore. *Internal Labor Markets and Manpower
Analysis*. Lexington, Mass.: D.C. Heath and Co.,1971.

Doeringer, Peter B. *Programs to Employ the Disadvantaged*. Englewood Cliffs,
N.J.: Prentice-Hall, 1969.

Drake, St. Clair, and Horace R. Cayton. *Black Metropolis*. New York: Harper
Torchbooks, 1962.

Duncan, Otis Dudley. "Inheritance of Poverty or Inheritance of Race?" *On
Understanding Poverty*. Edited by Daniel P. Moynihan. New York: Basic
Books, 1969.

Durbin, Elizabeth F. "The Labor Market for Poor People in New York City."
*Welfare, Income, and Employment: An Analysis of Family Choice.
Labor, Economics and Urban Studies*, Vol. 1. New York: Frederick A.
Praeger, 1969.

Economic Development Council of New York City, Inc. *New York City's
Publicly-Financed Manpower Programs—Structure and Function*. New
York: Economic Development Council of New York City, Inc., 1971.

"Employment Situation in Urban Poverty Neighborhoods. Third Quarter, 1970." *Black News Digest*, November 2, 1970.

Eppley, David B. "The AFDC Family in the 1960's." *Welfare in Review* 8 (September-October, 1970).

Epps, Edgar. *Motivation and Performance of Negro Students*. Ann Arbor: University of Michigan, Institute for Social Research, September 1966.

Epstein, Lenore A. "Measuring the Size of the Low Income Population." *Six Papers on the Size Distribution of Wealth and Income*. Edited by L. Soltow. New York: Columbia University Press, 1969.

Erickson, Edsel. "Differences Between Economically Disadvantaged Students Who Volunteer and Do Not Volunteer for Economic Opportunity Programs." *Journal of Human Resources* 4:1 (1969), 76-83.

Fearn, Robert M. "Labor Force and School Participation of Teenagers." (Ph.D. Dissertation, University of Chicago, 1968).

Ferman, Louis A. *Job Development for the Hard-to-Employ*. Ann Arbor: University of Michigan, Institute for Industry and Labor Relations, 1968.

Fine, Sidney A. *Guidelines for the Employment of the Culturally Disadvantaged*. Kalamazoo, Mich.: W.E. Upjohn Institute for Employment Research, 1969.

Fogel, Walter. "The Effect of Low Educational Attainment on Incomes: A Comparative Study of Selected Ethnic Groups." *Journal of Human Resources* 1 (1966), 22–40.

Folk, Hugh. "The Problems of Youth Unemployment." *The Transition from School to Work*. Princeton: Princeton University, 1968, pp. 76–107.

Frazier, E. Franklin. *The Negro Family in the United States*. Chicago: University of Chicago Press, 1966.

Freedman, Marcia. "The Prospect for Young Workers." *Manpower Strategy for the Metropolis*. Edited by Eli Ginzberg and the Conservation of Human Resources Staff of Columbia University. New York: Columbia University Press, 1968.

Frumkin, Norman. *Manpower Implications of Alternative Priorities for Coping with Poverty*. Washington, D.C.: Department of Labor, Manpower Administration, 1969.

Galloway, L.E. "Unemployment Levels Among Non-white Teenagers." *Journal of Business* 42:3 (1969), 265-76.

Gavett, Thomas. "Youth Unemployment and Minimum Wages." *Monthly Labor Review* 93 (1970), 3-12.

Geneva International Labor Office. *Special Youth Employment and Training Schemes for Development Purposes*. Switzerland: Geneva International Labor Office, 1968.

Ginzberg, Eli, and the Conservation of Human Resources Staff of Columbia University. *Manpower Strategy for the Metropolis*. New York: Columbia University Press, 1968.

Ginzberg, E., S.W. Ginzberg, S. Axelrod, and J.L. Harma. *Occupation Choice*. New York: Columbia University Press, 1951.

Glaser, Barney G., and Anselm L. Strauss. *Discovery of Grounded Theory: Strategies for Qualitative Research*. Chicago: Aldine Publishing Co., 1967.

Glazer, Nona Y., and Carol F. Creedon. *Children and Poverty: Some Sociological and Psychological Perspectives.* Chicago: Rand McNally, 1968.

Glover, Heather. "The Unemployed Drop-out, 16-18 Years Old." *Current Issues* 3 (1969), 14–29.

Goldstein, Bernard. *Low Income Youth in Urban Areas: A Critical Review of the Literature.* New York: Holt, Rinehart and Winston, 1967.

Goldwin, Irwin J., Roslyn G. MacDonald, and Joyce Epstein. "Characteristics of Jobs Held by Economically Disadvantaged Youth." *American Journal of Orthopsychiatry* 40 (January 1970), 97–105.

Goodman, Leonard H., and Myint, Thelma D. *The Economic Needs of Neighborhood Youth Corps Enrollees.* New York: Bureau of Social Science Research, Inc., 1969.

Goodwin, Leonard. *Do the Poor Want to Work?* Washington, D.C.: The Brookings Institution, 1972.

———. "Work Orientations of the Underemployed Poor: Report on a Pilot Study." *Journal of Human Resources* 4 (1969), 508-19.

Gordon, Jesse E. "Testing, Counseling and Supportive Services." *Breakthrough for Disadvantaged Youth.* Washington, D.C.: Department of Labor, Manpower Administration, 1969.

Gordon, Joan. *The Poor of Harlem: Social Functioning in the Underclass.* New York: Office of the Mayor, Interdepartmental Neighborhood Service Center, 1965.

Gordon, Robert, and Margaret S. Gordon, eds. *Prosperity and Unemployment.* New York: Wiley, 1966.

Groemping, Franz A. *Transition from School to Work in Selected Countries.* Washington, D.C.: Department of Labor, 1969.

Gross, Edward. "Elements for a Youth Employment Program for the U.S." *Creativity and Innovation in Manpower, Research, and Action Programs.* Edited by the Industrial Relations Center of Iowa State University. Ames: Iowa State University, 1970.

Gruber, Murray. "The Nonculture of Poverty Among Black Youths." *Social Work* 17:3 (1972).

Gurin, Gerald. *Inner-City Negro Youth in a Job Training Project: A Study of Factors Related to Attrition and Job Success.* Ann Arbor: University of Michigan, Survey Research Center, 1968.

Gurin, Gerald, and Particia Gurin. "Expectancy Theory in the Study of Poverty." *Journal of Social Issues* 26:2 (1970), 83–104.

Hall, Oswald, and Bruce McFarland. *Transition from School to Work.* Report No. 10. Washington, D.C.: Department of Labor, The Interdepartmental Skilled Manpower Training Committee, December, 1962.

Harlem Youth Opportunities Unlimited, Inc. *Youth in the Ghetto.* New York: HARYOU, 1964.

Harwood, Edwin. "Youth Unemployment—A Tale of Two Ghettos." *Public Interest,* Fall 1969, pp. 78-87.

———, and Robert Olasov. *Houston's Out-of-School Neighborhood Youth Corps.* Houston, Tex.: Rice University, Department of Anthropology and Sociology, 1968.

Haskell, Mark A. *The New Careers Concept: Potential for Public Employment of the Poor.* New York: Frederick A. Praeger, 1969.

Hayghe, Howard. *Employment of High School Graduates and Dropouts.* Special Labor Force Report No. 121. Washington, D.C.: Department of Labor, 1970.

Hedges, Janice Neipert. "Skilled Trades for Girls." *Occupational Outlook Quarterly,* December 1967, pp. 9–13.

Heneman, Herbert G., Jr., and Rene V. Dawes. "Youth Unemployment: Frictions in the Threshold of the Work Career—An Exploratory Probe." Minneapolis: University of Minnesota, n.d.

Herman, Melvin, Stanley Sadofsky, and Bernard Rosenberg. *Work, Youth, and Unemployment.* New York: Thomas V. Crowell Co., 1968.

"Heroin Addiction and Drug Abuse in New York." *City Almanac* 6:6 (April 1972).

Herzog, Elizabeth; Ceclia Sudia; Barbara Rosengard; and Jane Harwood. *Teenagers Discuss the "Generation Gap."* Youth Report No. 1. Washington, D.C.: Department of Health, Education, and Welfare, Office of Child Development, 1970.

Herzog, Elizabeth. "Family Structure and Composition: Research Considerations." *Race, Research, and Reason: Social Work Perspectives.* Edited by Roger R. Miller and Cecelia R. Sudia. New York: National Association of Social Workers, 1969.

――――. *About the Poor: Some Facts and Some Factors.* Washington, D.C.: Department of Health, Education, and Welfare, SRS, Children's Bureau, 1967.

――――. "Is There a 'Breakdown' of the Negro Family?" *Social Work* 11:1 (1966), 3–10.

Hiestand, Dale. "White Collar Employment Opportunities for Minorities in New York City." Mimeographed. Washington, D.C.: Office of Research and Reports, Equal Opportunity Commission, 1967.

Hill, Robert B. *The Strengths of Black Families.* New York: Emerson Hall Publishers, 1971.

Himes, Joseph S. "Some Work-Related Cultural Deprivations of Lower-Class Negro Youth." *Journal of Marriage and the Family* 26 (November 1964), 447-49.

Hodge, Claire C. *The Negro Job Situation: Has It Improved?* Special Labor Force Report No. 102. Washington, D.C.: Department of Labor, Office of Manpower and Employment Statistics, January 1969.

Holland, Daniel M. "An Evaluation of Tax Incentives for On-the-Job Training of the Disadvantaged." *The Bell Journal of Economics and Management Science* 2:1 (1971).

Holland, Dempsterk. "Underemployment: Key to Unemployment." *Urban and Social Change Review,* Spring 1970, pp. 20–22.

Holt, Charles C., *et al. The Unemployment-Inflation Dilemma: A Manpower Solution.* Washington, D.C.: The Urban Institute, 1971.

Human Resources Administration. *Opportunity Centers System Vols. 1, 2, and 3*. New York: Human Resources Administration, Manpower and Career Development Agency, 1970.

———. *The New York City Human Resources Administration Annual Report 1969*. New York: Human Resources Administration, 1969.

Information Center on Crime and Delinquency. National Council on Crime and Delinquency. *Selected References in Juvenile Delinquency and Youth Development*. Office of Juvenile Delinquency and Youth Development, Welfare Administration, Department of Health, Education, and Welfare, 1967.

Institute of Public Administration. *Developing New York City's Human Resources: Report of a Study Group of the Institute of Public Administration to Mayor John V. Lindsay*. New York: Institute of Public Administration, 1966.

Jeffers, Camille, *Living Poor: A Participant Observer Study of Priorities and Choices*. Ann Arbor: Ann Arbor Publishers, 1967.

———. *Three Generations. Case Materials in Low Income Urban Living*. Washington, D.C.: CROSS-TELL, 1966.

Kalachek, Edward. "Determinants of Teenage Employment." *Journal of Human Resources* 4:1 (1969).

———. *The Youth Labor Market*. Ann Arbor: University of Michigan-Wayne State University, Institute of Labor and Industrial Relations, 1969.

Kaufman, J.J., C.J. Shaefer, M.V. Lewis, D.W. Stevens, and E.W. House. *Role of the Secondary Schools in the Preparation of Youth for Employment*. University Park, Pa.: Pennsylvania State University, Institute for Research on Human Resources, 1967.

Kaufman, Richard F. "Youth Employment in the Slums: A Proposal for Change." *Employment Service Review*, October 1967, pp. 10–13.

Key, N.G. "Occupational Aspirations and Labor Force Experience of Negro Youth." *American Journal of Economics and Sociology*, April, 1969.

Keyserling, Mary Dublin. *Windows on Day Care*. New York: National Council of Jewish Women, 1972.

Kidder, Alice, and David Kidder. *Employment Creation Effects of Negro Business with Particular Emphasis on Negro Teenage Employment Potential*. Springfield, Va.: Department of Commerce, Federal Scientific and Technical Information, 1969.

Kidder, Alice. "Racial Differences in Job Search and Wages." *Monthly Labor Review*, July 1968, pp. 24-26.

Killingsworth, Charles C. *Rising Unemployment: A Transitional" Problem?* East Lansing: Michigan State University, School of Labor and Industrial Relations, 1970.

Kohler, Mary Conway, and Marcia Freedman. *Youth and Work in New York City*. New York: Taconic Foundation, Inc., 1962.

Korbel, John. "Female Labor Force Mobility and Its Stimulation." *Human Resources in the Urban Economy*. Edited by Mark Perlman. Washington, D.C.: Resources for the Future, Inc., 1963.

Kruger, Daniel H. *Minimum Wages and Youth Employment.* East Lansing:
    Michigan State University, School of Labor and Industrial Relations, 1970.
Ladner, Joyce A. *Tomorrow's Tomorrow: The Black Woman.* Garden City,
    N.Y.: Doubleday and Co., 1971.
Leshner, S., and G.S. Snyderman. "Preparing Disadvantaged Youth." *Employ-
    ment Service Review* 2:2 (1965), 53-55.
Levitan, Sar. *Economic Opportunity in the Ghetto.* Baltimore: Johns Hopkins
    Press, 1969.
Lewis, Hylan. "The Culture of Poverty: What Does It Matter?" *The Poor: A
    Culture of Poverty, or a Poverty of Culture?* Edited by J. Alan Winter.
    Grand Rapids, Mich.: William B. Eerdmans, 1971.
_____ and Elizabeth Herzog. "Children in Poor Families: Myths and Realities."
    American Journal of Orthopsychiatry 40:3 (1970), 375-87.
Lewis, Hylan. "Culture, Class and Family Life Among Low Income Urban
    Negroes." *Employment, Race, and Poverty.* Edited by Arthur M. Ross and
    Herbert Hill. New York: Harcourt, Brace and World, 1967.
_____ . *Culture, Class and Poverty.* Washington, D.C.: Health and Welfare
    Council of the National Capital Area, 1967.
_____ . "The Family: New Agenda, Different Rhetoric." *Children of Poverty –
    Children of Affluence.* New York: Child Study Association of America,
    1967.
_____ . "Syndromes of Contemporary Urban Poverty." *Psychiatric Research
    Report 21.* New York: American Psychiatric Association, April 1967.
_____ , and Elizabeth Herzog. "Priorities in Research on Unmarried Mothers."
    Research Perspectives on the Unmarried Mother. New York: Child Welfare
    League of America, Inc., 1962.
Lewis, Hylan. "Child Rearing Practices Among Low Income Families." *Case-
    work Papers, 1961.* New York: Family Service Association of America,
    1961.
_____ . "The Changing Negro Family." *The Nation's Children: The Family
    and Social Change.* Edited by Eli Ginzberg. New York: Columbia Univer-
    sity Press, 1960.
_____ . "Juvenile Delinquency Among Negroes: A Critical Summary."
    Journal of Negro Education, 1959.
Low, Seth, and Pearl G. Spindles. "Child Care Arrangements of Working
    Mothers in the U.S." Washington, D.C.: Department of Health, Education,
    and Welfare, and Department of Labor, 1968.
Lynden, Patricia. "What Day Care Means to the Children, the Parents, the
    Teachers, the Community, the President." *New York Times Magazine,*
    February 15, 1970, sec. 6.
McNally, Gertrude B. "Patterns of Female Labor Force Activity." *Industrial
    Relations,* May 1968, p. 204.
Mahoney, Thomas. "Factors Determining the Labor Force Participation of
    Married Women." *Industrial and Labor Relations Review,* July 1961,
    pp. 563–77.
Maloy, Richard J. "The Profit Motive: Can It Motivate Industry to Hire the
    Hard-Core?" *Manpower* 1:1 (1969).

Mandell, Wallace; Sheldon Blackman; and Clyde Sullivan. *Disadvantaged Youth Approaching the World of Work: A Study of NYC Enrollees in New York City, A Final Report.* Staten Island, N.Y.: Wakoff Research Center, 1969.

Mangum, Garth L. "Employment Opportunities and Job Development in the Inner City." *Employment and Manpower Problems in the Cities: Implications of the Report of the National Advisory Commission on Civil Disorders. Hearings* before the Joint Economic Committee, 90th Cong., 2d sess., 1968.

Marshall, Ray. "Trends in Black Income and Employment." *The American Federalist* 78:7 (1971).

————. *The Negro Worker.* New York: Random House, 1967.

Mayer, Anna B., and Alfred J. Kahn. *Day Care as a Social Instrument: A Policy Paper.* New York: Columbia University, School of Social Work, 1965.

Miller, Delbert C., and William H. Form. *Industrial Sociology.* New York: Harper College Books, 1964.

Miller, Seymour M., and Pamela A. Roby. *The Future of Inequality.* New York: Basic Books, 1970.

Miller, Seymour M. "The Outlook of Working Class Youth." *Blue-Collar World: Studies of the American Worker.* Edited by Arthur B. Shostak and William Gomberg. Englewood Cliffs, N.J.: Prentice-Hall, 1964.

Mincer, Jacob. "Labor Force Participation of Married Women: A Study of Labor Supply." *National Bureau of Economic Research, Aspects of Labor Economics.* Princeton: Princeton University Press, 1962.

Mirengoff, William, ed. *Breakthrough for Disadvantaged Youth.* Washington, D.C.: Department of Labor, Manpower Administration, 1969.

Mitchell, Robert B. *Jobs in Transition.* New York: Community Renewal Program, June, 1966.

Mobilization for Youth, Inc., and Columbia University School of Social Work. "The Youth Employment Problem: Some Findings and Implications." New York: Mobilization for Youth, Inc., n.d.

Mooney, Joseph D. "Urban Poverty and Labor Force Participation." *American Economic Review* 57:1 (1967).

————. "Teenage Labor Problems and the Neighborhood Youth Corps." *Critical Issues in Employment Policy.* Edited by Frederick Harbison and Joseph Mooney. A report of the Princeton Manpower Symposium, May 12-13, 1966. Princeton: Princeton University, 1966.

Morisey, Patricia Garland. "Illegitimacy—A Special Minority Group Problem in Urban Areas: New Social Welfare Perspectives." *Child Welfare* 45 (1966), 8.

————. "Family Strengths and Family Survival." *Proceedings from the Conference of New York State Branches, American Psychiatric Association.* New York City, November, 1967.

Morse, Dean W. "The Peripheral Worker in the Affluent Society." *Monthly Labor Review,* February 1968, p. 17.

————. "The Peripheral Worker." *Manpower Strategy for the Metropolis.* Edited by Eli Ginzberg and the Conservation of Human Resources Staff of Columbia University. New York: Columbia University Press, 1968.

National Board of the Young Women's Christian Association of the U.S.A. *Summer Youth Demonstration Project.* Vols. I and II. Washington, D.C.: Department of Labor, November 1967.

National Committee for Children and Youth. *Social Dynamite.* Report of the Conference on Unemployed Out-of-School Youth in Urban Areas. Washington, D.C.: National Committee for Children and Youth, 1961.

National Urban Coalition and the Lawyers' Committee for Civil Rights Under the Law. *Falling Down on the Job: The United States Employment Service and the Disadvantaged.* Washington, D.C.: National Urban Coalition and the Lawyers' Committee for Civil Rights Under the Law, 1971.

New York City. Bureau of Child Health. Division of Day Care. Day Camps and Institutions. *Day Care Services in Operation–December 1971.* Mimeographed.

New York City. Department of Health. *Directory of Day Care Services in New York City.* New York: Department of Health, New York City, 1971.

New York City Planning Commission. *Planning for Jobs.* New York: New York City Planning Commission, 1971.

New York State. Department of Labor. *Manpower Directions in New York State: 1965-1975.* Vol. I. Special Bulletin 241, March 1968.

Norwell, Reynolds I. "A Plan for Youth Employment." *The Disadvantaged Poor: Education and Employment.* Vol. III. Edited by the US Chamber of Commerce. Washington, D.C.: Chamber of Commerce, 1966.

Nye, F. Ivan, and Hoffman, Lois Wladis. *The Employed Mother In America.* Chicago: Rand McNally and Co., 1963.

Parnes, Herbert, Robert C. Miljus, Ruth S. Spitz, and Associates. *Career Thresholds: A Longitudinal Study of the Educational and Labor Market Experience of Male Youth 14–24 Years of Age.* Columbus: Ohio State University, Center for Human Resource Research, 1969.

Pearl, Arthur, and F. Reismann. *New Careers for the Poor.* New York: Free Press, 1965.

Perlmutter, Emanuel. "Metropolitan Area Loses 88,000 Jobs in a Year." *New York Times,* May 11, 1971. p. 1.

Piker, Jeffry. *Entry Into Labor Force: A Survey of Literature on the Experience of Negro and White Youths.* Ann Arbor: Wayne State University, Institute of Labor and Industrial Relations, University of Michigan, 1968.

Poussaint, Alvin F. "Negro Youth and Psychological Motivation." *Educating the Disadvantaged: School Year 1968-1969.* New York: AMS Press, 1970.

Powers, Mary G., and Gerald M. Shattuck. *The Job Supervisors Role in Neighborhood Youth Corps Programs for Out-of-School Youth in New York City.* New York: Fordham University, Institute for Social Research, 1970.

Powledge, Fred. *New Careers: Real Jobs and Opportunities for the Disadvantaged.* New York: Public Affairs Committee, 1968.

President's Council on Youth Opportunity. *Bridging the Gap from School to Work.* Reprint from *Manpower Report of the President.* Washington, D.C.: Government Printing Office, 1968.

Purnell, Richard F., and Gerald S. Lesser. "Work-Bound and College-Bound
    Youth: A Study in Stereotypes." Cambridge, Mass.: Harvard University,
    Laboratory of Human Development, n.d.
Rainwater, Lee. *Behind Ghetto Walls: Black Families in a Federal Slum*.
    Chicago: Aldine Publishing Co., 1970.
Rosenberg, M. *Society and the Adolescent Self-Image*. Princeton: Princeton
    University Press, 1965.
Ruttenberg, Stanley H. *Manpower Challenge of the 1970's Institutions and
    Social Change*. Baltimore: Johns Hopkins Press, 1970.
Schrank, Robert. "Feasibility in Youth Employment Programs." Paper pre-
    sented at the United Neighborhood Houses, 80th Conference, New York,
    N.Y., December 6, 1966.
Schreiber, David, ed. *Profile of the School Dropout*. New York: Random
    House, 1967.
Schulz, David A. "Coming Up as a Girl in the Ghetto." *Coming Up Black:
    Patterns of Ghetto Socialization*. Englewood Cliffs, N.J.: Prentice-Hall,
    1969.
Schwartz, M., and Henderson, G. "The Culture of Unemployment: Some
    Notes on Negro Children." *Blue-Collar World: Studies of the American
    Worker*. Edited by Arthur B. Shostak and William Gomberg. Englewood
    Cliffs, N.J.: Prentice-Hall, 1964.
Scully, Gerald W. "The Impact of Minimum Wages on the Unemployment
    Rates of Minority Group Labor." Athens, Ohio: Ohio University, 1970.
Seiler, Joseph. "Prevocational and Vocational Training Programs." *Break-
    through for Disadvantaged Youth*. Washington, D.C.: Department of
    Labor, Manpower Administration, 1969.
Sexton, Patricia Cayo. "Basic Education." *Breakthrough for Disadvantaged
    Youth*. Washington, D.C.: Department of Labor, Manpower Adminis-
    tration, 1969.
Shea, John, Roger D. Roderick, Frederick A. Zeller, and Andrew I. Kohen.
    *Years for Decision: A Longitudinal Study of the Educational and Labor
    Market Experience of Young Women*. Vol. I. Washington, D.C.: Govern-
    ment Printing Office, 1971.
Shostak, Arthur B., and Gomberg, William, eds. *Blue-Collar World: Studies
    of the American Worker*. Englewood Cliffs, N.J.: Prentice Hall, 1964.
Smith, Harold T. *Education and Training for the World of Work: A Voca-
    tional Education Program for the State of Michigan*. Kalamazoo, Mich.:
    W.E. Upjohn Institute for Employment Research, July, 1963.
Somers, Gerald G., and Ernest W. Stromsdorfer. "A Cost-Effectiveness
    Study of the In-School and Summer Neighborhood Youth Corps."
    Madison: University of Wisconsin, 1970.
Stagner, Ross. *Psychological Dynamics of Inner City Problems, Seminar on
    Manpower Policy and Program*. Washington, D.C.: Department of Labor,
    Manpower Administration, 1968.
Stein, Robert L. "The Economics Status of Families Headed by Women."
    Monthly Labor Review 93 (December 1970), 3–10.

Stevens, David W. *Supplemental Labor Market Information as a Means to Increase Effectiveness of Job Search Activity.* University Park, Pa.: Institute for Research on Human Resources, Pennsylvania State University, 1968.

Super, Donald E. "Vocational Development of High School Dropouts." *Guidance and the School Dropout.* Edited by Daniel Schreiber. Washington, D.C.: National Education Association, 1964, pp. 66-83.

————. *The Psychology of Careers.* New York: Harper, 1957.

Tabb, William K. "The Ghetto Worker and the Labor Market." *The Political Economy of the Black Ghetto.* New York: W.W. Norton and Co., 1970.

Tannenbaum, A.J. *Dropout or Diploma: A Socio-educational Analysis of Early School Withdrawal.* New York: Teachers College Press, Columbia University, 1966.

Thurow, Lester C. "The Determinants of the Occupational Distribution of Negroes." *Education and Training of Disadvantaged Minorities.* Edited by Gerald Somers. Madison: Wisconsin University Press, 1969.

"Trends in Social and Economic Conditions in Metropolitan and Nonmetropolitan Areas." *Current Population Reports Special Studies.* Series p-23, no. 33, September 3, 1970.

US Chamber of Commerce. Task Force on Economic Growth and Opportunity. *The Disadvantaged Poor: Education and Employment.* Washington, D.C.: Chamber of Commerce, Task Force on Economic Growth and Opportunity, 1966.

US Department of Commerce. Bureau of the Census. Census of Population 1970, Subject Reports. *Negro Population,* PC(2)-1B. Washington, D.C.: Government Printing Office, 1973.

————. *Employment Profiles of Selected Low-Income Areas.* Reports PHC(3)-7, 2, 4, 5, 7, 9. Washington, D.C.: Government Printing Office, 1972.

US Department of Health, Education, and Welfare and Department of Labor. *Child Care Arrangements of Working Mothers in the U.S.* Washington, D.C.: Department of Health, Education, and Welfare and Department of Labor, 1968.

US Department of Labor. *Manpower Report of the President.* Washington, D.C.: Government Printing Office, 1971-73.

————. *Automation and Women Workers.* Washington, D.C.: Government Printing Office, 1970.

————. *U.S. Manpower in the 1970's: Opportunity and Challenge.* Washington, D.C.: Government Printing Office, 1970.

————. *Disadvantaged Youth.* Washington, D.C.: Government Printing Office, June 1967.

————. *Neighborhood Youth Corps First National Conference Report.* Washington, D.C.: Government Printing Office, 1966.

US Department of Labor. Bureau of Labor Statistics. *The Economics of Working and Living in New York City.* New York: Department of Labor Statistics, Middle Atlantic Region, 1972.

_____. *1971 Year End Report on Jobs, Prices, and Earnings in the New York Area.* Regional Labor Statistics Bulletin No. 30. New York: Department of Labor Statistics, Middle Atlantic Region, 1971.

_____. *Poverty Area Profiles: Working Age Nonparticipants: Persons Not in the Labor Force and Their Employment Problems.* Regional Report No. 22. New York: Department of Labor, Bureau of Labor Statistics, 1971.

_____. *Some Facts Relating to the New York Scene.* New York: Department of Labor, Bureau of Labor Statistics, Middle Atlantic Regional Office, 1971.

_____. *Employment of High School Graduates and Dropouts.* Special Labor Force Report No. 121. Washington, D.C.: Government Printing Office, 1970.

_____. *Employment in Perspective: An Examination of Recent Developments in the Labor Force, Employment and Unemployment.* Washington, D.C.: Government Printing Office, 1970.

_____. *Long-Duration Unemployment.* Special Labor Force Report 118. Washington, D.C.: Department of Labor, Bureau of Labor Statistics, 1970.

_____. *Poverty Area Profiles: Characteristics of the Unemployed.* Regional Report No. 14. New York: Department of Labor, Bureau of Labor Statistics, 1970.

_____. *Regional Labor Statistics Bulletin: Year-end Report on Jobs, Prices, and Earnings in the New York Area.* New York: Department of Labor, Bureau of Labor Statistics, Middle Atlantic Region, December, 1970.

_____. *Youth Unemployment and Minimum Wages.* Bulletin 1657. Washington, D.C.: Government Printing Office, 1970.

_____. *Handbook of Labor Statistics, 1969.* Washington, D.C.: Government Printing Office, 1969.

_____. *A Sharper Look at Unemployment in U.S. Cities and Slums.* Washington, D.C.: Government Printing Office, 1966.

_____. *Sub-Employment in the Slums of New York.* Washington, D.C.: Government Printing Office, 1966.

_____. Manpower Administration. *The Neighborhood Youth Corps: A Review of Research.* Washington, D.C.: Government Printing Office, 1970.

_____. *Boys Residential Youth Center, Final Report.* New Haven, Conn.: Boys Residential Youth Center, 1969.

_____. *Girls Residential Youth Center. Final Report.* New Haven, Conn.: Girls Residential Youth Center, 1969.

_____. "Credentials and Common Sense Jobs for People without Diplomas." Washington, D.C.: Government Printing Office, 1968.

_____. Wage and Labor Standards Administration. *Negro Women . . . In the Population and in the Labor Force.* Washington, D.C.: Government Printing Office, 1968.

_____. Women's Bureau. *1969 Handbook on Women Workers.* Bulletin 294. Washington, D.C.: Government Printing Office, 1969.

US Equal Employment Commission. *Equal Employment Opportunity Report No. 1: Job Patterns for Minorities and Women in Private Industry 1966-1970.* Washington, D.C.: Government Printing Office, 1968-72.

US Office of Economic Opportunity. Office of Planning Research and Evalua-
    tion. *A Study of Day Care's Effect on the Labor Force Participation of
    Low-Income Mothers.* Edited by Jack Ditmore and W.R. Prosser. Washing-
    ton, D.C., June 1973.
————. Office of Planning Research and Evaluation. *Federal Youth Programs.*
    Washington, D.C., December 1972.
Venn, Grant. "Vocational-Technical Education Needs and Programs for Urban
    Schools." Paper presented at the Seventh Annual Work Conference on
    Urban Education, Teachers College, Columbia University, New York, N.Y.,
    June 23, 1969.
Waldman, Elizabeth. *Employment Status of School Age Youth, October 1968.*
    Special Labor Force Report No. 111. Washington, D.C.: Department of
    Labor, Bureau of Labor Statistics, August 1969.
Wallace, Phyllis A. "Employment Discrimination: Some Policy Considera-
    tions." Albert Rees and Orley Ashenfelter, editors. *Discrimination in
    Labor Markets.* Princeton: Princeton University Press, 1973.
————. "Employment Status of Black Women." Research in progress.
————. "Economic Position and Prospects for Urban Blacks." *American
    Journal of Agricultural Economics* 53:2 (1971).
————. "Discrimination: A Barrier to Effective Manpower Utilization."
    Proceedings of the Industrial Relations Research Associations, Winter 1967.
___, et al. "Testing of Minority Applicants for Employment." Research
    Report No. 7. Equal Employment Opportunity Commission, March
    1966.
Walther, Regis H. *A Study of Negro Male High School Drop-Outs Who Are Not
    Reached by Federal Work-Training Programs.* Washington, D.C.: George
    Washington University, Social Research Group, 1969.
————. *A Study of the Effectiveness of Selected Out-of-School Neighborhood
    Youth Corps Programs: Implications for Program Operations and Research.*
    Washington, D.C.: George Washington University, Social Research Group,
    1969.
————. *A Study of the Effectiveness of Selected Out-of-School Neighborhood
    Youth Corps Programs: The Measurement of Work-Relevant Attitudes.*
    Washington, D.C.: George Washington University, Social Research Group.
    1969.
Weissman, Harold H., ed. *Employment and Educational Services in the Mobili-
    zation for Youth Experience.* New York: Association Press, 1969.
Wells, Jean A. *Facts About Women's Absenteeism and Labor Turnover.* Wash-
    ington, D.C.: Department of Labor, Women's Bureau, 1969.
Willacy, H.M., and Hilaski, H.J. "Working Women in Urban Poverty Neighbor-
    hoods." *Monthly Labor Review* 93:6 (1970) :35–38.
*Work in America: Report of a Special Task Force to the Secretary of Health,
    Education, and Welfare.* Cambridge: MIT Press, 1973.
"Year-End Report on Jobs, Prices, and Earnings in the New York Area." *Labor
    Statistics Bulletin,* no. 25. New York: Department of Labor, Bureau of
    Labor Statistics, 1970.

Young, Anne M. *Employment of School-Age Youth.* Special Labor Force
    Report 124. Washington, D.C.: Department of Labor, Bureau of Labor
    Statistics, 1969.
Youth Work Program Review Staff of the National Committee on Employment
    of Youth. *Getting Hired, Getting Trained.* New York: National Committee
    on Employment of Youth, 1964.

Index

Index

About the Author

Phyllis A. Wallace received the Ph.D. in economics from Yale University and has served as senior economist for the U.S. Government. A member of the National Manpower Policy Task Force, Dr. Wallace is Visiting Professor of Management at the Alfred P. Sloan School of Management, Massachusetts Institute of Technology.